CAMBRIDGE

IELTS
ACADEMIC 16

WITH ANSWERS

AUTHENTIC PRACTICE TESTS

Cambridge University Press
www.cambridge.org/elt

Cambridge Assessment English
www.cambridgeenglish.org

Information on this title: www.cambridge.org/9781108933858

© Cambridge University Press and Cambridge Assessment 2021

First published 2021

20 19 18 17 16 15 14 13 12 11 10 9 8 7 6 5 4 3

Printed in Malaysia by Vivar Printing

A catalogue record for this publication is available from the British Library

ISBN 978-1-108-93385-8 Academic Student's Book with Answers with Audio
ISBN 978-1-108-93386-5 General Training Student's Book with Answers with Audio

Contents

Introduction

Prepare for the exam with practice tests from Cambridge

Inside you'll find four authentic examination papers from Cambridge Assessment English. They are the perfect way to practise – EXACTLY like the real exam.

Why are they unique?

All our authentic practice tests go through the same design process as the IELTS test. We check every single part of our practice tests with real students under exam conditions, to make sure we give you the most authentic experience possible.

Students can practise these tests on their own or with the help of a teacher to familiarise themselves with the exam format, understand the scoring system and practise exam technique.

Further information

IELTS is jointly managed by the British Council, IDP: IELTS Australia and Cambridge Assessment English. Further information can be found on the IELTS official website at ielts.org.

WHAT IS THE TEST FORMAT?

IELTS consists of four components. All candidates take the same Listening and Speaking tests. There is a choice of Reading and Writing tests according to whether a candidate is taking the Academic or General Training module.

Academic	General Training
For candidates wishing to study at undergraduate or postgraduate levels, and for those seeking professional registration.	For candidates wishing to migrate to an English-speaking country (Australia, Canada, New Zealand, UK), and for those wishing to train or study below degree level.

The test components are taken in the following order:

Listening 4 parts, 40 items, approximately 30 minutes		
Academic Reading 3 sections, 40 items 60 minutes	or	**General Training Reading** 3 sections, 40 items 60 minutes
Academic Writing 2 tasks 60 minutes	or	**General Training Writing** 2 tasks 60 minutes
Speaking 11 to 14 minutes		
Total Test Time 2 hours 44 minutes		

ACADEMIC TEST FORMAT

Listening

This test consists of four parts, each with ten questions. The first two parts are concerned with social needs. The first part is a conversation between two speakers and the second part is a monologue. The final two parts are concerned with situations related to educational or training contexts. The third part is a conversation between up to four people and the fourth part is a monologue.

A variety of question types is used, including: multiple choice, matching, plan/map/ diagram labelling, form completion, note completion, table completion, flow-chart completion, summary completion, sentence completion and short-answer questions.

Candidates hear the recording once only and answer the questions as they listen. Ten minutes are allowed at the end for candidates to transfer their answers to the answer sheet.

Reading

This test consists of three sections with 40 questions. There are three texts, which are taken from journals, books, magazines and newspapers. The texts are on topics of general interest. At least one text contains detailed logical argument.

A variety of question types is used, including: multiple choice, identifying information (True/False/Not Given), identifying the writer's views/claims (Yes/No/Not Given), matching information, matching headings, matching features, matching sentence endings, sentence completion, summary completion, note completion, table completion, flow-chart completion, diagram-label completion and short-answer questions.

Writing

This test consists of two tasks. It is suggested that candidates spend about 20 minutes on Task 1, which requires them to write at least 150 words, and 40 minutes on Task 2, which requires them to write at least 250 words. Task 2 contributes twice as much as Task 1 to the Writing score.

Task 1 requires candidates to look at a diagram or some data (in a graph, table or chart) and to present the information in their own words. They are assessed on their ability to organise, present and possibly compare data, and are required to describe the stages of a process, describe an object or event, or explain how something works.

In Task 2, candidates are presented with a point of view, argument or problem. They are assessed on their ability to present a solution to the problem, present and justify an opinion, compare and contrast evidence and opinions, and to evaluate and challenge ideas, evidence or arguments.

Candidates are also assessed on their ability to write in an appropriate style. More information on assessing the Writing test, including Writing assessment criteria (public version), is available at ielts.org.

Speaking

This test takes between 11 and 14 minutes and is conducted by a trained examiner. There are three parts:

Part 1

The candidate and the examiner introduce themselves. Candidates then answer general questions about themselves, their home/family, their job/studies, their interests and a wide range of similar familiar topic areas. This part lasts between four and five minutes.

Part 2

The candidate is given a task card with prompts and is asked to talk on a particular topic. The candidate has one minute to prepare and they can make some notes if they wish, before speaking for between one and two minutes. The examiner then asks one or two questions on the same topic.

Part 3

The examiner and the candidate engage in a discussion of more abstract issues which are thematically linked to the topic in Part 2. The discussion lasts between four and five minutes.

The Speaking test assesses whether candidates can communicate effectively in English. The assessment takes into account Fluency and Coherence, Lexical Resource, Grammatical Range and Accuracy, and Pronunciation. More information on assessing the Speaking test, including Speaking assessment criteria (public version), is available at ielts.org.

HOW IS IELTS SCORED?

IELTS results are reported on a nine-band scale. In addition to the score for overall language ability, IELTS provides a score in the form of a profile for each of the four skills (Listening, Reading, Writing and Speaking). These scores are also reported on a nine-band scale. All scores are recorded on the Test Report Form along with details of the candidate's nationality, first language and date of birth. Each Overall Band Score corresponds to a descriptive statement which gives a summary of the English-language ability of a candidate classified at that level. The nine bands and their descriptive statements are as follows:

9   *Expert user – Has fully operational command of the language: appropriate, accurate and fluent with complete understanding.*

8   *Very good user – Has fully operational command of the language with only occasional unsystematic inaccuracies and inappropriacies. Misunderstandings may occur in unfamiliar situations. Handles complex detailed argumentation well.*

7   *Good user – Has operational command of the language, though with occasional inaccuracies, inappropriacies and misunderstandings in some situations. Generally handles complex language well and understands detailed reasoning.*

6   *Competent user – Has generally effective command of the language despite some inaccuracies, inappropriacies and misunderstandings. Can use and understand fairly complex language, particularly in familiar situations.*

5   *Modest user – Has partial command of the language, coping with overall meaning in most situations, though is likely to make many mistakes. Should be able to handle basic communication in own field.*

4   *Limited user – Basic competence is limited to familiar situations. Has frequent problems in understanding and expression. Is not able to use complex language.*

3   *Extremely limited user – Conveys and understands only general meaning in very familiar situations. Frequent breakdowns in communication occur.*

2   *Intermittent user – Has great difficulty understanding spoken and written English.*

1   *Non-user – Essentially has no ability to use the language beyond possibly a few isolated words.*

0   *Did not attempt the test – Did not answer the questions.*

MARKING THE PRACTICE TESTS

Listening and Reading

The answer keys are on pages 121–128.
Each question in the Listening and Reading tests is worth one mark.

Questions which require letter / Roman numeral answers

For questions where the answers are letters or Roman numerals, you should write *only* the number of answers required. For example, if the answer is a single letter or numeral, you should write only one answer. If you have written more letters or numerals than are required, the answer must be marked wrong.

Questions which require answers in the form of words or numbers

- Answers may be written in upper or lower case.
- Words in brackets are *optional* – they are correct, but not necessary.
- Alternative answers are separated by a slash (/).
- If you are asked to write an answer using a certain number of words and/or (a) number(s), you will be penalised if you exceed this. For example, if a question specifies an answer using NO MORE THAN THREE WORDS and the correct answer is 'black leather coat', the answer 'coat of black leather' is *incorrect*.
- In questions where you are expected to complete a gap, you should only transfer the necessary missing word(s) onto the answer sheet. For example, to complete 'in the …', where the correct answer is 'morning', the answer 'in the morning' would be *incorrect*.
- All answers require correct spelling (including words in brackets).
- Both US and UK spelling are acceptable and are included in the answer key.
- All standard alternatives for numbers, dates and currencies are acceptable.
- All standard abbreviations are acceptable.
- You will find additional notes about individual answers in the answer key.

Writing

The sample answers are on pages 129–138. It is not possible for you to give yourself a mark for the Writing tasks. We have provided sample answers (written by candidates), showing their score and the examiners' comments. These sample answers will give you an insight into what is required for the Writing test.

HOW SHOULD YOU INTERPRET YOUR SCORES?

At the end of each Listening and Reading answer key you will find a chart which will help you assess whether, on the basis of your Practice Test results, you are ready to take the IELTS test.

In interpreting your score, there are a number of points you should bear in mind. Your performance in the real IELTS test will be reported in two ways: there will be a Band Score from 1 to 9 for each of the components and an Overall Band Score from 1 to 9, which is the average of your scores in the four components. However, institutions considering your application are advised to look at both the Overall Band Score and the Band Score for each component in order to determine whether you have the language skills needed for a particular course of study. For example, if your course involves a lot of reading and writing, but no lectures, listening skills might be less important and a score of 5 in Listening might be acceptable if the Overall Band Score was 7. However, for a course which has lots of lectures and spoken instructions, a score of 5 in Listening might be unacceptable even though the Overall Band Score was 7.

Once you have marked your tests, you should have some idea of whether your listening and reading skills are good enough for you to try the IELTS test. If you did well enough in one component, but not in others, you will have to decide for yourself whether you are ready to take the test.

The Practice Tests have been checked to ensure that they are the same level of difficulty as the real IELTS test. However, we cannot guarantee that your score in the Practice Tests will be reflected in the real IELTS test. The Practice Tests can only give you an idea of your possible future performance and it is ultimately up to you to make decisions based on your score.

Different institutions accept different IELTS scores for different types of courses. We have based our recommendations on the average scores which the majority of institutions accept. The institution to which you are applying may, of course, require a higher or lower score than most other institutions.

Test 1

PART 1   *Questions 1–10*

Complete the notes below.

*Write **ONE WORD AND/OR A NUMBER** for each answer.*

Listening test audio

Children's Engineering Workshops

Tiny Engineers (ages 4–5)

Activities

- Create a cover for an **1** .... so they can drop it from a height without breaking it.

- Take part in a competition to build the tallest **2** ....

- Make a **3** .... powered by a balloon.

Junior Engineers (ages 6–8)

Activities:

- Build model cars, trucks and **4** .... and learn how to program them so they can move.

- Take part in a competition to build the longest **5** .... using card and wood.

- Create a short **6** .... with special software.

- Build, **7** .... and program a humanoid robot.

Cost for a five-week block: £50

Held on **8** .... from 10 am to 11 am

Location

Building 10A, **9** .... Industrial Estate, Grasford

Plenty of **10** .... is available.

PART 2   *Questions 11–20*

Questions 11–14

*Choose the correct letter, **A**, **B** or **C**.*

Listening test audio

11 Stevenson's was founded in

   A   1923.
   B   1924.
   C   1926.

12 Originally, Stevenson's manufactured goods for

   A   the healthcare industry.
   B   the automotive industry.
   C   the machine tools industry.

13 What does the speaker say about the company premises?

   A   The company has recently moved.
   B   The company has no plans to move.
   C   The company is going to move shortly.

14 The programme for the work experience group includes

   A   time to do research.
   B   meetings with a teacher.
   C   talks by staff.

Questions 15–20

Label the map below.

*Write the correct letter, **A–J**, next to Questions 15–20.*

Plan of Stevenson's site

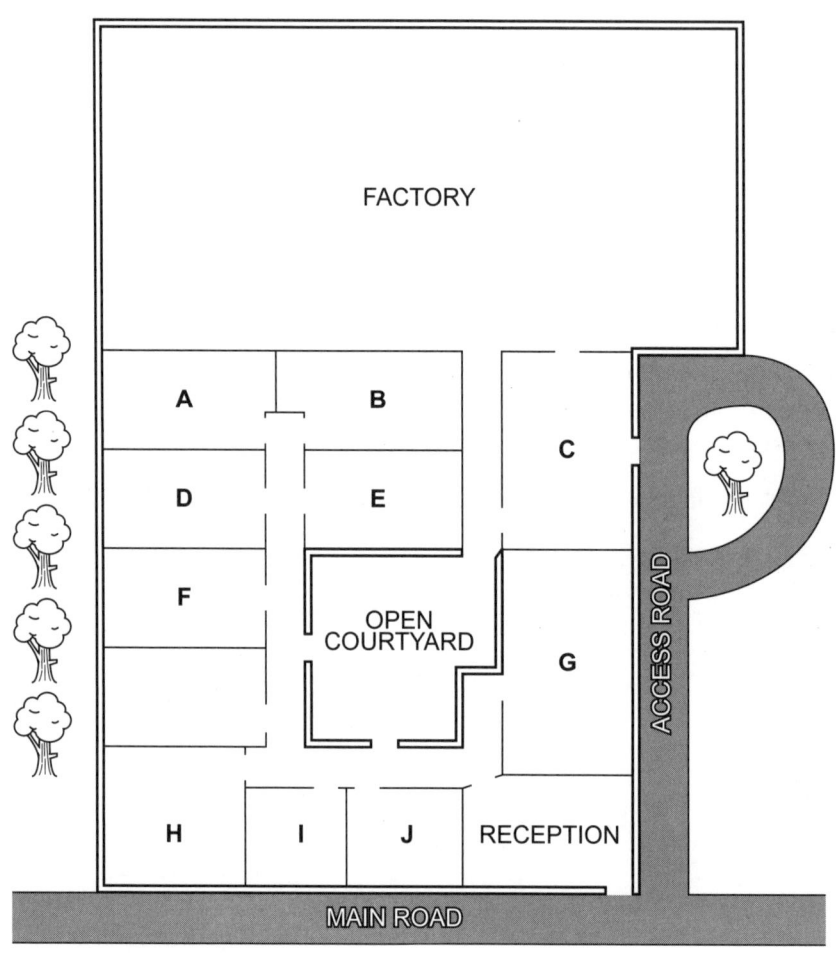

15	coffee room	....
16	warehouse	....
17	staff canteen	....
18	meeting room	....
19	human resources	....
20	boardroom	....

PART 3   *Questions 21–30*

Listening test audio

Questions 21 and 22

*Choose **TWO** letters, **A–E**.*

Which **TWO** parts of the introductory stage to their art projects do Jess and Tom agree were useful?

    A   the Bird Park visit
    B   the workshop sessions
    C   the Natural History Museum visit
    D   the projects done in previous years
    E   the handouts with research sources

Questions 23 and 24

*Choose **TWO** letters, **A–E**.*

In which **TWO** ways do both Jess and Tom decide to change their proposals?

    A   by giving a rationale for their action plans
    B   by being less specific about the outcome
    C   by adding a video diary presentation
    D   by providing a timeline and a mind map
    E   by making their notes more evaluative

Questions 25–30

Which personal meaning do the students decide to give to each of the following pictures?

*Choose **SIX** answers from the box and write the correct letter, **A–H**, next to Questions 25–30.*

Personal meanings
A   a childhood memory
B   hope for the future
C   fast movement
D   a potential threat
E   the power of colour
F   the continuity of life
G   protection of nature
H   a confused attitude to nature

Pictures

25   Falcon (Landseer)   ....

26   Fish hawk (Audubon)   ....

27   Kingfisher (van Gogh)   ....

28   Portrait of William Wells   ....

29   Vairumati (Gauguin)   ....

30   Portrait of Giovanni de Medici   ....

PART 4   *Questions 31–40*

Complete the notes below.

*Write **ONE WORD ONLY** for each answer.*

Listening test audio

Stoicism

Stoicism is still relevant today because of its **31** .... appeal.

Ancient Stoics

* Stoicism was founded over 2,000 years ago in Greece.
* The Stoics' ideas are surprisingly well known, despite not being intended for **32** ....

Stoic principles

* Happiness could be achieved by leading a virtuous life.
* Controlling emotions was essential.
* Epictetus said that external events cannot be controlled but the **33** .... people make in response can be controlled.
* A Stoic is someone who has a different view on experiences which others would consider as **34** ....

The influence of Stoicism

* George Washington organised a **35** .... about Cato to motivate his men.
* The French artist Delacroix was a Stoic.
* Adam Smith's ideas on **36** .... were influenced by Stoicism.
* Some of today's political leaders are inspired by the Stoics.
* Cognitive Behaviour Therapy (CBT)

  – the treatment for **37** .... is based on ideas from Stoicism

  – people learn to base their thinking on **38** ....
* In business, people benefit from Stoicism by identifying obstacles as **39** ....

Relevance of Stoicism

* It requires a lot of **40** .... but Stoicism can help people to lead a good life.
* It teaches people that having a strong character is more important than anything else.

READING PASSAGE 1

*You should spend about 20 minutes on **Questions 1–13,** which are based on Reading Passage 1 below.*

Why we need to protect polar bears

Polar bears are being increasingly threatened by the effects of climate change, but their disappearance could have far-reaching consequences. They are uniquely adapted to the extreme conditions of the Arctic Circle, where temperatures can reach −40°C. One reason for this is that they have up to 11 centimetres of fat underneath their skin. Humans with comparative levels of adipose tissue would be considered obese and would be likely to suffer from diabetes and heart disease. Yet the polar bear experiences no such consequences.

A 2014 study by Shi Ping Liu and colleagues sheds light on this mystery. They compared the genetic structure of polar bears with that of their closest relatives from a warmer climate, the brown bears. This allowed them to determine the genes that have allowed polar bears to survive in one of the toughest environments on Earth. Liu and his colleagues found the polar bears had a gene known as APoB, which reduces levels of low-density lipoproteins (LDLs) – a form of 'bad' cholesterol. In humans, mutations of this gene are associated with increased risk of heart disease. Polar bears may therefore be an important study model to understand heart disease in humans.

The genome of the polar bear may also provide the solution for another condition, one that particularly affects our older generation: osteoporosis. This is a disease where bones show reduced density, usually caused by insufficient exercise, reduced calcium intake or food starvation. Bone tissue is constantly being remodelled, meaning that bone is added or removed, depending on nutrient availability and the stress that the bone is under. Female polar bears, however, undergo extreme conditions during every pregnancy. Once autumn comes around, these females will dig maternity dens in the snow and will remain there throughout the winter, both before and after the birth of their cubs. This process results in about six months of fasting, where the female bears have to keep themselves and their cubs alive, depleting their own calcium and calorie reserves. Despite this, their bones remain strong and dense.

Physiologists Alanda Lennox and Allen Goodship found an explanation for this paradox in 2008. They discovered that pregnant bears were able to increase the density of their bones before they started to build their dens. In addition, six months later, when they finally emerged from the den with their cubs, there was no evidence of significant loss of bone density. Hibernating brown bears do not have this capacity and must therefore resort to major bone reformation in the following spring. If the mechanism of bone remodelling in polar bears can be understood, many bedridden humans, and even astronauts, could potentially benefit.

The medical benefits of the polar bear for humanity certainly have their importance in our conservation efforts, but these should not be the only factors taken into consideration. We tend to want to protect animals we think are intelligent and possess emotions, such as elephants and primates. Bears, on the other hand, seem to be perceived as stupid and in many cases violent. And yet anecdotal evidence from the field challenges those assumptions, suggesting for example that polar bears have good problem-solving abilities. A male bear called GoGo in Tennoji Zoo, Osaka, has even been observed making use of a tool to manipulate his environment. The bear used a tree branch on multiple occasions to dislodge a piece of meat hung out of his reach. Problem-solving ability has also been witnessed in wild polar bears, although not as obviously as with GoGo. A calculated move by a male bear involved running and jumping onto barrels in an attempt to get to a photographer standing on a platform four metres high.

In other studies, such as one by Alison Ames in 2008, polar bears showed deliberate and focussed manipulation. For example, Ames observed bears putting objects in piles and then knocking them over in what appeared to be a game. The study demonstrates that bears are capable of agile and thought-out behaviours. These examples suggest bears have greater creativity and problem-solving abilities than previously thought.

As for emotions, while the evidence is once again anecdotal, many bears have been seen to hit out at ice and snow – seemingly out of frustration – when they have just missed out on a kill. Moreover, polar bears can form unusual relationships with other species, including playing with the dogs used to pull sleds in the Arctic. Remarkably, one hand-raised polar bear called Agee has formed a close relationship with her owner Mark Dumas to the point where they even swim together. This is even more astonishing since polar bears are known to actively hunt humans in the wild.

If climate change were to lead to their extinction, this would mean the loss not only of potential breakthroughs in human medicine, but more importantly, the disappearance of an intelligent, majestic animal.

Test 1

Questions 1–7

Do the following statements agree with the information given in Reading Passage 1?

In boxes 1–7 on your answer sheet, write

>**TRUE**   *if the statement agrees with the information*
>**FALSE**   *if the statement contradicts the information*
>**NOT GIVEN**   *if there is no information on this*

1   Polar bears suffer from various health problems due to the build-up of fat under their skin.

2   The study done by Liu and his colleagues compared different groups of polar bears.

3   Liu and colleagues were the first researchers to compare polar bears and brown bears genetically.

4   Polar bears are able to control their levels of 'bad' cholesterol by genetic means.

5   Female polar bears are able to survive for about six months without food.

6   It was found that the bones of female polar bears were very weak when they came out of their dens in spring.

7   The polar bear's mechanism for increasing bone density could also be used by people one day.

Questions 8–13

Complete the table below.

*Choose **ONE WORD ONLY** from the passage for each answer.*

Write your answers in boxes 8–13 on your answer sheet.

Reasons why polar bears should be protected

People think of bears as unintelligent and **8** ....

However, this may not be correct. For example:

- In Tennoji Zoo, a bear has been seen using a branch as a **9** .... This allowed him to knock down some **10** ....

- A wild polar bear worked out a method of reaching a platform where a **11** .... was located.

- Polar bears have displayed behaviour such as conscious manipulation of objects and activity similar to a **12** ....

Bears may also display emotions. For example:

- They may make movements suggesting **13** .... if disappointed when hunting.

- They may form relationships with other species.

READING PASSAGE 2

You should spend about 20 minutes on **Questions 14–26**, *which are based on Reading Passage 2 on pages 21 and 22.*

Questions 14–20

Reading Passage 2 has seven paragraphs, **A–G**.

Choose the correct heading for each paragraph from the list of headings below.

Write the correct number, **i–ix**, *in boxes 14–20 on your answer sheet.*

List of Headings

   i   The areas and artefacts within the pyramid itself

  ii   A difficult task for those involved

 iii   A king who saved his people

  iv   A single certainty among other less definite facts

   v   An overview of the external buildings and areas

  vi   A pyramid design that others copied

 vii   An idea for changing the design of burial structures

viii   An incredible experience despite the few remains

  ix   The answers to some unexpected questions

---

14   Paragraph **A**

15   Paragraph **B**

16   Paragraph **C**

17   Paragraph **D**

18   Paragraph **E**

19   Paragraph **F**

20   Paragraph **G**

The Step Pyramid of Djoser

A The pyramids are the most famous monuments of ancient Egypt and still hold enormous interest for people in the present day. These grand, impressive tributes to the memory of the Egyptian kings have become linked with the country even though other cultures, such as the Chinese and Mayan, also built pyramids. The evolution of the pyramid form has been written and argued about for centuries. However, there is no question that, as far as Egypt is concerned, it began with one monument to one king designed by one brilliant architect: the Step Pyramid of Djoser at Saqqara.

B Djoser was the first king of the Third Dynasty of Egypt and the first to build in stone. Prior to Djoser's reign, tombs were rectangular monuments made of dried clay brick, which covered underground passages where the deceased person was buried. For reasons which remain unclear, Djoser's main official, whose name was Imhotep, conceived of building a taller, more impressive tomb for his king by stacking stone slabs on top of one another, progressively making them smaller, to form the shape now known as the Step Pyramid. Djoser is thought to have reigned for 19 years, but some historians and scholars attribute a much longer time for his rule, owing to the number and size of the monuments he built.

C The Step Pyramid has been thoroughly examined and investigated over the last century, and it is now known that the building process went through many different stages. Historian Marc Van de Mieroop comments on this, writing 'Much experimentation was involved, which is especially clear in the construction of the pyramid in the center of the complex. It had several plans ... before it became the first Step Pyramid in history, piling six levels on top of one another ... The weight of the enormous mass was a challenge for the builders, who placed the stones at an inward incline in order to prevent the monument breaking up.'

D When finally completed, the Step Pyramid rose 62 meters high and was the tallest structure of its time. The complex in which it was built was the size of a city in ancient Egypt and included a temple, courtyards, shrines, and living quarters for the priests. It covered a region of 16 hectares and was surrounded by a wall 10.5 meters high. The wall had 13 false doors cut into it with only one true entrance cut into the south-east corner; the entire wall was then ringed by a trench 750 meters long and 40 meters wide. The false doors and the trench were incorporated into the complex to discourage unwanted visitors. If someone wished to enter, he or she would have needed to know in advance how to find the location of the true opening in the wall. Djoser was so proud of his accomplishment that he broke the tradition of having only his own name on the monument and had Imhotep's name carved on it as well.

E   The burial chamber of the tomb, where the king's body was laid to rest, was dug beneath the base of the pyramid, surrounded by a vast maze of long tunnels that had rooms off them to discourage robbers. One of the most mysterious discoveries found inside the pyramid was a large number of stone vessels. Over 40,000 of these vessels, of various forms and shapes, were discovered in storerooms off the pyramid's underground passages. They are inscribed with the names of rulers from the First and Second Dynasties of Egypt and made from different kinds of stone. There is no agreement among scholars and archaeologists on why the vessels were placed in the tomb of Djoser or what they were supposed to represent. The archaeologist Jean-Philippe Lauer, who excavated most of the pyramid and complex, believes they were originally stored and then given a 'proper burial' by Djoser in his pyramid to honor his predecessors. There are other historians, however, who claim the vessels were dumped into the shafts as yet another attempt to prevent grave robbers from getting to the king's burial chamber.

F   Unfortunately, all of the precautions and intricate design of the underground network did not prevent ancient robbers from finding a way in. Djoser's grave goods, and even his body, were stolen at some point in the past and all archaeologists found were a small number of his valuables overlooked by the thieves. There was enough left throughout the pyramid and its complex, however, to astonish and amaze the archaeologists who excavated it.

G   Egyptologist Miroslav Verner writes, 'Few monuments hold a place in human history as significant as that of the Step Pyramid in Saqqara … It can be said without exaggeration that this pyramid complex constitutes a milestone in the evolution of monumental stone architecture in Egypt and in the world as a whole.' The Step Pyramid was a revolutionary advance in architecture and became the archetype which all the other great pyramid builders of Egypt would follow.

Questions 21–24

Complete the notes below.

*Choose **ONE WORD ONLY** from the passage for each answer.*

Write your answers in boxes 21–24 on your answer sheet.

The Step Pyramid of Djoser

The complex that includes the Step Pyramid and its surroundings is considered to be as big as an Egyptian **21** .... of the past. The area outside the pyramid included accommodation that was occupied by **22** .... , along with many other buildings and features.

A wall ran around the outside of the complex and a number of false entrances were built into this. In addition, a long **23** .... encircled the wall. As a result, any visitors who had not been invited were cleverly prevented from entering the pyramid grounds unless they knew the **24** .... of the real entrance.

Questions 25–26

*Choose **TWO** letters, **A–E**.*

Write the correct letters in boxes 25 and 26 on your answer sheet.

Which **TWO** of the following points does the writer make about King Djoser?

    A   Initially he had to be persuaded to build in stone rather than clay.
    B   There is disagreement concerning the length of his reign.
    C   He failed to appreciate Imhotep's part in the design of the Step Pyramid.
    D   A few of his possessions were still in his tomb when archaeologists found it.
    E   He criticised the design and construction of other pyramids in Egypt.

➔ ◐ p. 122   23

READING PASSAGE 3

*You should spend about 20 minutes on **Questions 27–40**, which are based on Reading Passage 3 below.*

The future of work

According to a leading business consultancy, 3–14% of the global workforce will need to switch to a different occupation within the next 10–15 years, and all workers will need to adapt as their occupations evolve alongside increasingly capable machines. Automation – or 'embodied artificial intelligence' (AI) – is one aspect of the disruptive effects of technology on the labour market. 'Disembodied AI', like the algorithms running in our smartphones, is another.

Dr Stella Pachidi from Cambridge Judge Business School believes that some of the most fundamental changes are happening as a result of the 'algorithmication' of jobs that are dependent on data rather than on production – the so-called knowledge economy. Algorithms are capable of learning from data to undertake tasks that previously needed human judgement, such as reading legal contracts, analysing medical scans and gathering market intelligence.

'In many cases, they can outperform humans,' says Pachidi. 'Organisations are attracted to using algorithms because they want to make choices based on what they consider is "perfect information", as well as to reduce costs and enhance productivity.'

'But these enhancements are not without consequences,' says Pachidi. 'If routine cognitive tasks are taken over by AI, how do professions develop their future experts?' she asks. 'One way of learning about a job is "legitimate peripheral participation" – a novice stands next to experts and learns by observation. If this isn't happening, then you need to find new ways to learn.'

Another issue is the extent to which the technology influences or even controls the workforce. For over two years, Pachidi monitored a telecommunications company. 'The way telecoms salespeople work is through personal and frequent contact with clients, using the benefit of experience to assess a situation and reach a decision. However, the company had started using a[n] … algorithm that defined when account managers should contact certain customers about which kinds of campaigns and what to offer them.'

The algorithm – usually built by external designers – often becomes the keeper of knowledge, she explains. In cases like this, Pachidi believes, a short-sighted view begins to creep into working practices whereby workers learn through the 'algorithm's eyes' and become dependent on its instructions. Alternative explorations – where experimentation and human instinct lead to progress and new ideas – are effectively discouraged.

Pachidi and colleagues even observed people developing strategies to make the algorithm work to their own advantage. 'We are seeing cases where workers feed the algorithm with false data to reach their targets,' she reports.

It's scenarios like these that many researchers are working to avoid. Their objective is to make AI technologies more trustworthy and transparent, so that organisations and individuals understand how AI decisions are made. In the meantime, says Pachidi, 'We need to make sure we fully understand the dilemmas that this new world raises regarding expertise, occupational boundaries and control.'

Economist Professor Hamish Low believes that the future of work will involve major transitions across the whole life course for everyone: 'The traditional trajectory of full-time education followed by full-time work followed by a pensioned retirement is a thing of the past,' says Low. Instead, he envisages a multistage employment life: one where retraining happens across the life course, and where multiple jobs and no job happen by choice at different stages.

On the subject of job losses, Low believes the predictions are founded on a fallacy: 'It assumes that the number of jobs is fixed. If in 30 years, half of 100 jobs are being carried out by robots, that doesn't mean we are left with just 50 jobs for humans. The number of jobs will increase: we would expect there to be 150 jobs.'

Dr Ewan McGaughey, at Cambridge's Centre for Business Research and King's College London, agrees that 'apocalyptic' views about the future of work are misguided. 'It's the laws that restrict the supply of capital to the job market, not the advent of new technologies that causes unemployment.'

His recently published research answers the question of whether automation, AI and robotics will mean a 'jobless future' by looking at the causes of unemployment. 'History is clear that change can mean redundancies. But social policies can tackle this through retraining and redeployment.'

He adds: 'If there is going to be change to jobs as a result of AI and robotics then I'd like to see governments seizing the opportunity to improve policy to enforce good job security. We can "reprogramme" the law to prepare for a fairer future of work and leisure.' McGaughey's findings are a call to arms to leaders of organisations, governments and banks to pre-empt the coming changes with bold new policies that guarantee full employment, fair incomes and a thriving economic democracy.

'The promises of these new technologies are astounding. They deliver humankind the capacity to live in a way that nobody could have once imagined,' he adds. 'Just as the industrial revolution brought people past subsistence agriculture, and the corporate revolution enabled mass production, a third revolution has been pronounced. But it will not only be one of technology. The next revolution will be social.'

Questions 27–30

*Choose the correct letter, **A**, **B**, **C** or **D**.*

Write the correct letter in boxes 27–30 on your answer sheet.

27 The first paragraph tells us about

    A the kinds of jobs that will be most affected by the growth of AI.
    B the extent to which AI will alter the nature of the work that people do.
    C the proportion of the world's labour force who will have jobs in AI in the future.
    D the difference between ways that embodied and disembodied AI will impact on workers.

28 According to the second paragraph, what is Stella Pachidi's view of the 'knowledge economy'?

    A It is having an influence on the number of jobs available.
    B It is changing people's attitudes towards their occupations.
    C It is the main reason why the production sector is declining.
    D It is a key factor driving current developments in the workplace.

29 What did Pachidi observe at the telecommunications company?

    A staff disagreeing with the recommendations of AI
    B staff feeling resentful about the intrusion of AI in their work
    C staff making sure that AI produces the results that they want
    D staff allowing AI to carry out tasks they ought to do themselves

30 In his recently published research, Ewan McGaughey

    A challenges the idea that redundancy is a negative thing.
    B shows the profound effect of mass unemployment on society.
    C highlights some differences between past and future job losses.
    D illustrates how changes in the job market can be successfully handled.

Questions 31–34

*Complete the summary using the list of words, **A–G**, below.*

*Write the correct letter, **A–G**, in boxes 31–34 on your answer sheet.*

The 'algorithmication' of jobs

Stella Pachidi of Cambridge Judge Business School has been focusing on the 'algorithmication' of jobs which rely not on production but on **31** ....

While monitoring a telecommunications company, Pachidi observed a growing **32** .... on the recommendations made by AI, as workers begin to learn through the 'algorithm's eyes'. Meanwhile, staff are deterred from experimenting and using their own **33** .... , and are therefore prevented from achieving innovation.

To avoid the kind of situations which Pachidi observed, researchers are trying to make AI's decision-making process easier to comprehend, and to increase users' **34** .... with regard to the technology.

A	pressure	**B**	satisfaction	**C**	intuition
D	promotion	**E**	reliance	**F**	confidence
G	information				

Questions 35–40

Look at the following statements (Questions 35–40) and the list of people below.

*Match each statement with the correct person, **A**, **B** or **C**.*

*Write the correct letter, **A**, **B** or **C**, in boxes 35–40 on your answer sheet.*

***NB** You may use any letter more than once.*

35   Greater levels of automation will not result in lower employment.

36   There are several reasons why AI is appealing to businesses.

37   AI's potential to transform people's lives has parallels with major cultural shifts which occurred in previous eras.

38   It is important to be aware of the range of problems that AI causes.

39   People are going to follow a less conventional career path than in the past.

40   Authorities should take measures to ensure that there will be adequately paid work for everyone.

List of people
A   Stella Pachidi
B   Hamish Low
C   Ewan McGaughey

WRITING TASK 1

You should spend about 20 minutes on this task.

> *The charts below show the changes in ownership of electrical appliances and amount of time spent doing housework in households in one country between 1920 and 2019.*
>
> *Summarise the information by selecting and reporting the main features, and make comparisons where relevant.*

Write at least 150 words.

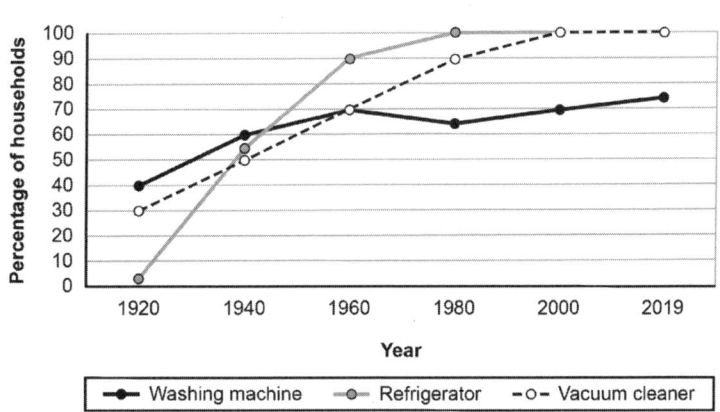

Percentage of households with electrical appliances (1920–2019)

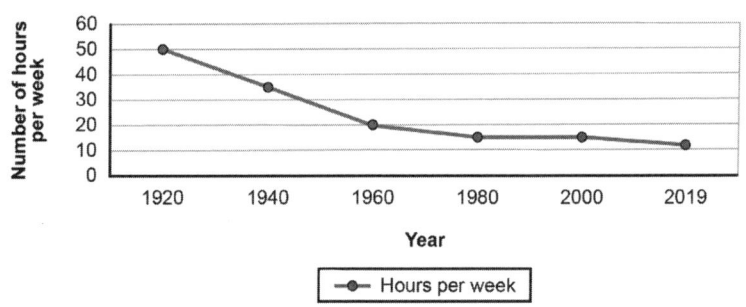

Number of hours of housework* per week, per household (1920–2019)

*housework = washing clothes, preparing meals, cleaning

WRITING TASK 2

You should spend about 40 minutes on this task.

Write about the following topic:

> *In some countries, more and more people are becoming interested in finding out about the history of the house or building they live in.*
>
> *What are the reasons for this?*
>
> *How can people research this?*

Give reasons for your answer and include any relevant examples from your own knowledge or experience.

Write at least 250 words.

PART 1

The examiner asks you about yourself, your home, work or studies and other familiar topics.

Example Speaking test video

EXAMPLE

People you study/work with

- Who do you spend most time studying/working with? [Why?]
- What kinds of things do you study / work on with other people? [Why?]
- Are there times when you study/work better by yourself? [Why/Why not?]
- Is it important to like the people you study/work with? [Why/Why not?]

PART 2

Describe a tourist attraction you enjoyed visiting.

You should say:
    what this tourist attraction is
    when and why you visited it
    what you did there

and explain why you enjoyed visiting this tourist attraction.

You will have to talk about the topic for one to two minutes. You have one minute to think about what you are going to say. You can make some notes to help you if you wish.

PART 3

Discussion topics:

Different kinds of tourist attractions

Example questions:
What are the most popular tourist attractions in your country?
How do the types of tourist attractions that younger people like to visit compare with those that older people like to visit?
Do you agree that some tourist attractions (e.g. national museums/galleries) should be free to visit?

The importance of international tourism

Example questions:
Why is tourism important to a country?
What are the benefits to individuals of visiting another country as tourists?
How necessary is it for tourists to learn the language of the country they're visiting?

Test 2

PART 1   Questions 1–10

Complete the notes below.

Write ONE WORD AND/OR A NUMBER for each answer.

Listening test audio

Copying photos to digital format

Name of company: Picturerep

Requirements

- Maximum size of photos is 30 cm, minimum size 4 cm.
- Photos must not be in a **1** .... or an album.

Cost

- The cost for 360 photos is **2** £ .... (including one disk).
- Before the completed order is sent, **3** .... is required.

Services included in the price

- Photos can be placed in a folder, e.g. with the name **4** ....
- The **5** .... and contrast can be improved if necessary.
- Photos which are very fragile will be scanned by **6** ....

Special restore service (costs extra)

- It may be possible to remove an object from a photo, or change the
  7 ....
- A photo which is not correctly in **8** .... cannot be fixed.

Other information

- Orders are completed within **9** ....
- Send the photos in a box (not **10** ....).

PART 2   *Questions 11–20*

Questions 11–15

Choose the correct letter, A, B or C.

Listening test audio

11   Dartfield House school used to be

    A   a tourist information centre.
    B   a private home.
    C   a local council building.

12   What is planned with regard to the lower school?

    A   All buildings on the main site will be improved.
    B   The lower school site will be used for new homes.
    C   Additional school buildings will be constructed on the lower school site.

13   The catering has been changed because of

    A   long queuing times.
    B   changes to the school timetable.
    C   dissatisfaction with the menus.

14   Parents are asked to

    A   help their children to decide in advance which serving point to use.
    B   make sure their children have enough money for food.
    C   advise their children on healthy food to eat.

15   What does the speaker say about the existing canteen?

    A   Food will still be served there.
    B   Only staff will have access to it.
    C   Pupils can take their food into it.

Questions 16–18

What comment does the speaker make about each of the following serving points in the Food Hall?

*Choose **THREE** answers from the box and write the correct letter, **A–D**, next to Questions 16–18.*

Comments
A   pupils help to plan menus
B   only vegetarian food
C   different food every week
D   daily change in menu

Food available at serving points in Food Hall

16   World Adventures   ....

17   Street Life   ....

18   Speedy Italian   ....

Questions 19 and 20

*Choose **TWO** letters, **A–E**.*

Which **TWO** optional after-school lessons are new?

    A   swimming
    B   piano
    C   acting
    D   cycling
    E   theatre sound and lighting

PART 3   *Questions 21–30*

Questions 21–24

*Choose the correct letter, **A**, **B** or **C**.*

Listening test audio

Assignment on sleep and dreams

21 Luke read that one reason why we often forget dreams is that

    A   our memories cannot cope with too much information.
    B   we might otherwise be confused about what is real.
    C   we do not think they are important.

22 What do Luke and Susie agree about dreams predicting the future?

    A   It may just be due to chance.
    B   It only happens with certain types of event.
    C   It happens more often than some people think.

23 Susie says that a study on pre-school children having a short nap in the day

    A   had controversial results.
    B   used faulty research methodology.
    C   failed to reach any clear conclusions.

24 In their last assignment, both students had problems with

    A   statistical analysis.
    B   making an action plan.
    C   self-assessment.

Test 2

Questions 25–30

Complete the flow chart below.

*Write **ONE WORD ONLY** for each answer.*

Assignment plan

Decide on research question:
Is there a relationship between hours of sleep and number of dreams?

↓

Decide on sample:
Twelve students from the **25** .... department

↓

Decide on methodology:
Self-reporting

↓

Decide on procedure:
Answers on **26** ....

↓

Check ethical guidelines for working with **27** ....
Ensure that risk is assessed and **28** .... is kept to a minimum

↓

Analyse the results
Calculate the correlation and make a **29** ....

↓

30 .... the research

PART 4   *Questions 31–40*

Complete the notes below.

Write ONE WORD ONLY for each answer.

Listening test audio

Health benefits of dance

Recent findings:

- All forms of dance produce various hormones associated with feelings of happiness.

- Dancing with others has a more positive impact than dancing alone.

- An experiment on university students suggested that dance increases **31** ....

- For those with mental illness, dance could be used as a form of **32** ....

Benefits of dance for older people:

- accessible for people with low levels of **33** ....

- reduces the risk of heart disease

- better **34** .... reduces the risk of accidents

- improves **35** .... function by making it work faster

- improves participants' general well-being

- gives people more **36** .... to take exercise

- can lessen the feeling of **37** .... , very common in older people

Benefits of Zumba:

- A study at The University of Wisconsin showed that doing Zumba for 40 minutes uses up as many **38** .... as other quite intense forms of exercise.

- The *American Journal of Health Behavior* study showed that:

  – women suffering from **39** .... benefited from doing Zumba.

  – Zumba became a **40** .... for the participants.

READING PASSAGE 1

*You should spend about 20 minutes on **Questions 1–13**, which are based on Reading Passage 1 below.*

The White Horse of Uffington

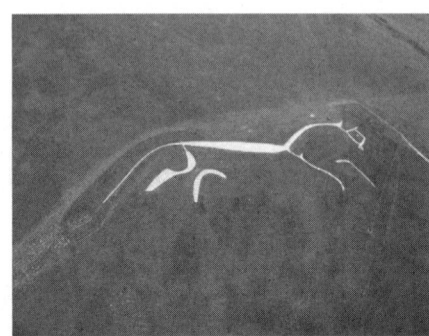

The cutting of huge figures or 'geoglyphs' into the earth of English hillsides has taken place for more than 3,000 years. There are 56 hill figures scattered around England, with the vast majority on the chalk downlands of the country's southern counties. The figures include giants, horses, crosses and regimental badges. Although the majority of these geoglyphs date within the last 300 years or so, there are one or two that are much older.

The most famous of these figures is perhaps also the most mysterious – the Uffington White Horse in Oxfordshire. The White Horse has recently been re-dated and shown to be even older than its previously assigned ancient pre-Roman Iron Age* date. More controversial is the date of the enigmatic Long Man of Wilmington in Sussex. While many historians are convinced the figure is prehistoric, others believe that it was the work of an artistic monk from a nearby priory and was created between the 11th and 15th centuries.

The method of cutting these huge figures was simply to remove the overlying grass to reveal the gleaming white chalk below. However, the grass would soon grow over the geoglyph again unless it was regularly cleaned or scoured by a fairly large team of people. One reason that the vast majority of hill figures have disappeared is that when the traditions associated with the figures faded, people no longer bothered or remembered to clear away the grass to expose the chalk outline. Furthermore, over hundreds of years the outlines would sometimes change due to people not always cutting in exactly the same place, thus creating a different shape to the original geoglyph. The fact that any ancient hill figures survive at all in England today is testament to the strength and continuity of local customs and beliefs which, in one case at least, must stretch back over millennia.

---

*Iron Age: a period (in Britain 800 BCE – 43 CE) that is characterised by the use of iron tools

The Uffington White Horse is a unique, stylised representation of a horse consisting of a long, sleek back, thin disjointed legs, a streaming tail, and a bird-like beaked head. The elegant creature almost melts into the landscape. The horse is situated 2.5 km from Uffington village on a steep slope close to the Late Bronze Age* (c. 7th century BCE) hillfort of Uffington Castle and below the Ridgeway, a long-distance Neolithic** track.

The Uffington Horse is also surrounded by Bronze Age burial mounds. It is not far from the Bronze Age cemetery of Lambourn Seven Barrows, which consists of more than 30 well-preserved burial mounds. The carving has been placed in such a way as to make it extremely difficult to see from close quarters, and like many geoglyphs is best appreciated from the air. Nevertheless, there are certain areas of the Vale of the White Horse, the valley containing and named after the enigmatic creature, from which an adequate impression may be gained. Indeed on a clear day the carving can be seen from up to 30 km away.

The earliest evidence of a horse at Uffington is from the 1070s CE when 'White Horse Hill' is mentioned in documents from the nearby Abbey of Abingdon, and the first reference to the horse itself is soon after, in 1190 CE. However, the carving is believed to date back much further than that. Due to the similarity of the Uffington White Horse to the stylised depictions of horses on 1st century BCE coins, it had been thought that the creature must also date to that period.

However, in 1995 Optically Stimulated Luminescence (OSL) testing was carried out by the Oxford Archaeological Unit on soil from two of the lower layers of the horse's body, and from another cut near the base. The result was a date for the horse's construction somewhere between 1400 and 600 BCE – in other words, it had a Late Bronze Age or Early Iron Age origin.

The latter end of this date range would tie the carving of the horse in with occupation of the nearby Uffington hillfort, indicating that it may represent a tribal emblem marking the land of the inhabitants of the hillfort. Alternatively, the carving may have been carried out during a Bronze or Iron Age ritual. Some researchers see the horse as representing the Celtic*** horse goddess Epona, who was worshipped as a protector of horses, and for her associations with fertility. However, the cult of Epona was not imported from Gaul (France) until around the first century CE. This date is at least six centuries after the Uffington Horse was probably carved. Nevertheless, the horse had great ritual and economic significance during the Bronze and Iron Ages, as attested by its depictions on jewellery and other metal objects. It is possible that the carving represents a goddess in native mythology, such as Rhiannon, described in later Welsh mythology as a beautiful woman dressed in gold and riding a white horse.

The fact that geoglyphs can disappear easily, along with their associated rituals and meaning, indicates that they were never intended to be anything more than temporary gestures. But this does not lessen their importance. These giant carvings are a fascinating glimpse into the minds of their creators and how they viewed the landscape in which they lived.

---

*Bronze Age: a period (in Britain c. 2,500 BCE – 800 BCE) that is characterised by the development of bronze tools

**Neolithic: a period (in Britain c. 4,000 BCE – c. 2,500 BCE) that is significant for the spread of agricultural practices, and the use of stone tools

***Celtic: an ancient people who migrated from Europe to Britain before the Romans

Test 2

Questions 1–8

Do the following statements agree with the information given in Reading Passage 1?

In boxes 1–8 on your answer sheet, write

> **TRUE**   *if the statement agrees with the information*
> **FALSE**   *if the statement contradicts the information*
> **NOT GIVEN**   *if there is no information on this*

1   Most geoglyphs in England are located in a particular area of the country.

2   There are more geoglyphs in the shape of a horse than any other creature.

3   A recent dating of the Uffington White Horse indicates that people were mistaken about its age.

4   Historians have come to an agreement about the origins of the Long Man of Wilmington.

5   Geoglyphs were created by people placing white chalk on the hillside.

6   Many geoglyphs in England are no longer visible.

7   The shape of some geoglyphs has been altered over time.

8   The fame of the Uffington White Horse is due to its size.

Questions 9–13

Complete the notes below.

*Choose **ONE WORD ONLY** from the passage for each answer.*

Write your answers in boxes 9–13 on your answer sheet.

The Uffington White Horse

The location of the Uffington White Horse:

• a distance of 2.5 km from Uffington village

• near an ancient road known as the **9** ....

• close to an ancient cemetery that has a number of burial mounds

Dating the Uffington White Horse:

• first reference to White Horse Hill appears in **10** .... from the 1070s

• horses shown on coins from the period 100 BCE – 1 BCE are similar in appearance

• according to analysis of the surrounding **11** .... , the Horse is Late Bronze Age / Early Iron Age

Possible reasons for creation of the Uffington White Horse:

• an emblem to indicate land ownership

• formed part of an ancient ritual

• was a representation of goddess Epona – associated with protection of horses and **12** ....

• was a representation of a Welsh goddess called **13** ....

READING PASSAGE 2

*You should spend about 20 minutes on **Questions 14–26**, which are based on Reading Passage 2 below.*

I contain multitudes

Wendy Moore reviews Ed Yong's book about microbes

Microbes, most of them bacteria, have populated this planet since long before animal life developed and they will outlive us. Invisible to the naked eye, they are ubiquitous. They inhabit the soil, air, rocks and water and are present within every form of life, from seaweed and coral to dogs and humans. And, as Yong explains in his utterly absorbing and hugely important book, we mess with them at our peril.

Every species has its own colony of microbes, called a 'microbiome', and these microbes vary not only between species but also between individuals and within different parts of each individual. What is amazing is that while the number of human cells in the average person is about 30 trillion, the number of microbial ones is higher – about 39 trillion. At best, Yong informs us, we are only 50 per cent human. Indeed, some scientists even suggest we should think of each species and its microbes as a single unit, dubbed a 'holobiont'.

In each human there are microbes that live only in the stomach, the mouth or the armpit and by and large they do so peacefully. So 'bad' microbes are just microbes out of context. Microbes that sit contentedly in the human gut (where there are more microbes than there are stars in the galaxy) can become deadly if they find their way into the bloodstream. These communities are constantly changing too. The right hand shares just one sixth of its microbes with the left hand. And, of course, we are surrounded by microbes. Every time we eat, we swallow a million microbes in each gram of food; we are continually swapping microbes with other humans, pets and the world at large.

It's a fascinating topic and Yong, a young British science journalist, is an extraordinarily adept guide. Writing with lightness and panache, he has a knack of explaining complex science in terms that are both easy to understand and totally enthralling. Yong is on a mission. Leading us gently by the hand, he takes us into the world of microbes – a bizarre, alien planet – in a bid to persuade us to love them as much as he does. By the end, we do.

For most of human history we had no idea that microbes existed. The first man to see these extraordinarily potent creatures was a Dutch lens-maker called Antony van Leeuwenhoek in the 1670s. Using microscopes of his own design that could magnify up to 270 times, he examined a drop of water from a nearby lake and found it teeming with tiny creatures he called 'animalcules'. It wasn't until nearly two hundred years later that the research of French biologist Louis Pasteur indicated that some microbes caused disease. It was Pasteur's 'germ theory' that gave bacteria the poor image that endures today.

Yong's book is in many ways a plea for microbial tolerance, pointing out that while fewer than one hundred species of bacteria bring disease, many thousands more play a vital role in maintaining our health. The book also acknowledges that our attitude towards bacteria is not a simple one. We tend to see the dangers posed by bacteria, yet at the same time we are sold yoghurts and drinks that supposedly nurture 'friendly' bacteria. In reality, says Yong, bacteria should not be viewed as either friends or foes, villains or heroes. Instead we should realise we have a symbiotic relationship, that can be mutually beneficial or mutually destructive.

What then do these millions of organisms do? The answer is pretty much everything. New research is now unravelling the ways in which bacteria aid digestion, regulate our immune systems, eliminate toxins, produce vitamins, affect our behaviour and even combat obesity. 'They actually help us become who we are,' says Yong. But we are facing a growing problem. Our obsession with hygiene, our overuse of antibiotics and our unhealthy, low-fibre diets are disrupting the bacterial balance and may be responsible for soaring rates of allergies and immune problems, such as inflammatory bowel disease (IBD).

The most recent research actually turns accepted norms upside down. For example, there are studies indicating that the excessive use of household detergents and antibacterial products actually destroys the microbes that normally keep the more dangerous germs at bay. Other studies show that keeping a dog as a pet gives children early exposure to a diverse range of bacteria, which may help protect them against allergies later.

The readers of Yong's book must be prepared for a decidedly unglamorous world. Among the less appealing case studies is one about a fungus that is wiping out entire populations of frogs and that can be halted by a rare microbial bacterium. Another is about squid that carry luminescent bacteria that protect them against predators. However, if you can overcome your distaste for some of the investigations, the reasons for Yong's enthusiasm become clear. The microbial world is a place of wonder. Already, in an attempt to stop mosquitoes spreading dengue fever – a disease that infects 400 million people a year – mosquitoes are being loaded with a bacterium to block the disease. In the future, our ability to manipulate microbes means we could construct buildings with useful microbes built into their walls to fight off infections. Just imagine a neonatal hospital ward coated in a specially mixed cocktail of microbes so that babies get the best start in life.

Questions 14–16

*Choose the correct letter, **A**, **B**, **C** or **D**.*

Write the correct letter in boxes 14–16 on your answer sheet.

14 What point does the writer make about microbes in the first paragraph?

    A   They adapt quickly to their environment.
    B   The risk they pose has been exaggerated.
    C   They are more plentiful in animal life than plant life.
    D   They will continue to exist for longer than the human race.

15 In the second paragraph, the writer is impressed by the fact that

    A   each species tends to have vastly different microbes.
    B   some parts of the body contain relatively few microbes.
    C   the average individual has more microbial cells than human ones.
    D   scientists have limited understanding of how microbial cells behave.

16 What is the writer doing in the fifth paragraph?

    A   explaining how a discovery was made
    B   comparing scientists' theories about microbes
    C   describing confusion among scientists
    D   giving details of how microbes cause disease

Questions 17–20

*Complete the summary using the list of words, **A–H**, below.*

*Write the correct letter, **A–H**, in boxes 17–20 on your answer sheet.*

We should be more tolerant of microbes

Yong's book argues that we should be more tolerant of microbes. Many have a beneficial effect, and only a relatively small number lead to **17** .... And although it is misleading to think of microbes as 'friendly', we should also stop thinking of them as the enemy. In fact, we should accept that our relationship with microbes is one based on **18** ....

New research shows that microbes have numerous benefits for humans. Amongst other things, they aid digestion, remove poisons, produce vitamins and may even help reduce obesity. However, there is a growing problem. Our poor **19** .... , our overuse of antibiotics, and our excessive focus on **20** .... are upsetting the bacterial balance and may be contributing to the huge increase in allergies and immune system problems.

A solution	**B** partnership	**C** destruction
D exaggeration	**E** cleanliness	**F** regulations
G illness	**H** nutrition	

Questions 21–26

Do the following statements agree with the claims of the writer in Reading Passage 2?

In boxes 21–26 on your answer sheet, write

YES	*if the statement agrees with the claims of the writer*
NO	*if the statement contradicts the claims of the writer*
NOT GIVEN	*if it is impossible to say what the writer thinks about this*

21 It is possible that using antibacterial products in the home fails to have the desired effect.

22 It is a good idea to ensure that children come into contact with as few bacteria as possible.

23 Yong's book contains more case studies than are necessary.

24 The case study about bacteria that prevent squid from being attacked may have limited appeal.

25 Efforts to control dengue fever have been surprisingly successful.

26 Microbes that reduce the risk of infection have already been put inside the walls of some hospital wards.

READING PASSAGE 3

*You should spend about 20 minutes on **Questions 27–40**, which are based on Reading Passage 3 below.*

How to make wise decisions

Across cultures, wisdom has been considered one of the most revered human qualities. Although the truly wise may seem few and far between, empirical research examining wisdom suggests that it isn't an exceptional trait possessed by a small handful of bearded philosophers after all – in fact, the latest studies suggest that most of us have the ability to make wise decisions, given the right context.

'It appears that experiential, situational, and cultural factors are even more powerful in shaping wisdom than previously imagined,' says Associate Professor Igor Grossmann of the University of Waterloo in Ontario, Canada. 'Recent empirical findings from cognitive, developmental, social, and personality psychology cumulatively suggest that people's ability to reason wisely varies dramatically across experiential and situational contexts. Understanding the role of such contextual factors offers unique insights into understanding wisdom in daily life, as well as how it can be enhanced and taught.'

It seems that it's not so much that some people simply possess wisdom and others lack it, but that our ability to reason wisely depends on a variety of external factors. 'It is impossible to characterize thought processes attributed to wisdom without considering the role of contextual factors,' explains Grossmann. 'In other words, wisdom is not solely an "inner quality" but rather unfolds as a function of situations people happen to be in. Some situations are more likely to promote wisdom than others.'

Coming up with a definition of wisdom is challenging, but Grossmann and his colleagues have identified four key characteristics as part of a framework of wise reasoning. One is intellectual humility or recognition of the limits of our own knowledge, and another is appreciation of perspectives wider than the issue at hand. Sensitivity to the possibility of change in social relations is also key, along with compromise or integration of different attitudes and beliefs.

Grossmann and his colleagues have also found that one of the most reliable ways to support wisdom in our own day-to-day decisions is to look at scenarios from a third-party perspective, as though giving advice to a friend. Research suggests that when adopting a first-person viewpoint we focus on 'the focal features of the environment' and when we adopt a third-person, 'observer' viewpoint we reason more broadly and focus more on interpersonal and moral ideals such as justice and impartiality. Looking at problems from this more expansive viewpoint appears to foster cognitive processes related to wise decisions.

What are we to do, then, when confronted with situations like a disagreement with a spouse or negotiating a contract at work, that require us to take a personal stake? Grossmann argues that even when we aren't able to change the situation, we can still evaluate these experiences from different perspectives.

For example, in one experiment that took place during the peak of a recent economic recession, graduating college seniors were asked to reflect on their job prospects. The students were instructed to imagine their career either 'as if you were a distant observer' or 'before your own eyes as if you were right there'. Participants in the group assigned to the 'distant observer' role displayed more wisdom-related reasoning (intellectual humility and recognition of change) than did participants in the control group.

In another study, couples in long-term romantic relationships were instructed to visualize an unresolved relationship conflict either through the eyes of an outsider or from their own perspective. Participants then discussed an incident with their partner for 10 minutes, after which they wrote down their thoughts about it. Couples in the 'other's eyes' condition were significantly more likely to rely on wise reasoning – recognizing others' perspectives and searching for a compromise – compared to the couples in the egocentric condition.

'Ego-decentering promotes greater focus on others and enables a bigger picture, conceptual view of the experience, affording recognition of intellectual humility and change,' says Grossmann.

We might associate wisdom with intelligence or particular personality traits, but research shows only a small positive relationship between wise thinking and crystallized intelligence and the personality traits of openness and agreeableness. 'It is remarkable how much people can vary in their wisdom from one situation to the next, and how much stronger such contextual effects are for understanding the relationship between wise judgment and its social and affective outcomes as compared to the generalized "traits",' Grossmann explains. 'That is, knowing how wisely a person behaves in a given situation is more informative for understanding their emotions or likelihood to forgive [or] retaliate as compared to knowing whether the person may be wise "in general".'

Questions 27–30

*Choose the correct letter, **A**, **B**, **C** or **D**.*

Write the correct letter in boxes 27–30 on your answer sheet.

27 What point does the writer make in the first paragraph?

  A Wisdom appears to be unique to the human race.
  B A basic assumption about wisdom may be wrong.
  C Concepts of wisdom may depend on the society we belong to.
  D There is still much to be discovered about the nature of wisdom.

28 What does Igor Grossmann suggest about the ability to make wise decisions?

  A It can vary greatly from one person to another.
  B Earlier research into it was based on unreliable data.
  C The importance of certain influences on it was underestimated.
  D Various branches of psychology define it according to their own criteria.

29 According to the third paragraph, Grossmann claims that the level of wisdom an individual shows

  A can be greater than they think it is.
  B will be different in different circumstances.
  C may be determined by particular aspects of their personality.
  D should develop over time as a result of their life experiences.

30 What is described in the fifth paragraph?

  A a difficulty encountered when attempting to reason wisely
  B an example of the type of person who is likely to reason wisely
  C a controversial view about the benefits of reasoning wisely
  D a recommended strategy that can help people to reason wisely

Questions 31–35

*Complete the summary using the list of words, **A–J**, below.*

*Write the correct letter, **A–J**, in boxes 31–35 on your answer sheet.*

The characteristics of wise reasoning

Igor Grossmann and colleagues have established four characteristics which enable us to make wise decisions. It is important to have a certain degree of **31** .... regarding the extent of our knowledge, and to take into account **32** .... which may not be the same as our own. We should also be able to take a broad **33** .... of any situation. Another key characteristic is being aware of the likelihood of alterations in the way that people relate to each other.

Grossmann also believes that it is better to regard scenarios with **34** .... By avoiding the first-person perspective, we focus more on **35** .... and on other moral ideals, which in turn leads to wiser decision-making.

A	opinions	**B**	confidence	**C**	view
D	modesty	**E**	problems	**F**	objectivity
G	fairness	**H**	experiences	**I**	range
J	reasons				

Questions 36–40

Do the following statements agree with the information given in Reading Passage 3?

In boxes 36–40 on your answer sheet, write

> **TRUE**　　　*if the statement agrees with the information*
> **FALSE**　　　*if the statement contradicts the information*
> **NOT GIVEN**　*if there is no information on this*

36 Students participating in the job prospects experiment could choose one of two perspectives to take.

37 Participants in the couples experiment were aware that they were taking part in a study about wise reasoning.

38 In the couples experiments, the length of the couples' relationships had an impact on the results.

39 In both experiments, the participants who looked at the situation from a more detached viewpoint tended to make wiser decisions.

40 Grossmann believes that a person's wisdom is determined by their intelligence to only a very limited extent.

→ 🔊 p. 124 51

WRITING

WRITING TASK 1

You should spend about 20 minutes on this task.

> **The diagram below shows the manufacturing process for making sugar from sugar cane.**
>
> **Summarise the information by selecting and reporting the main features, and make comparisons where relevant.**

Write at least 150 words.

How sugar is produced from sugar cane

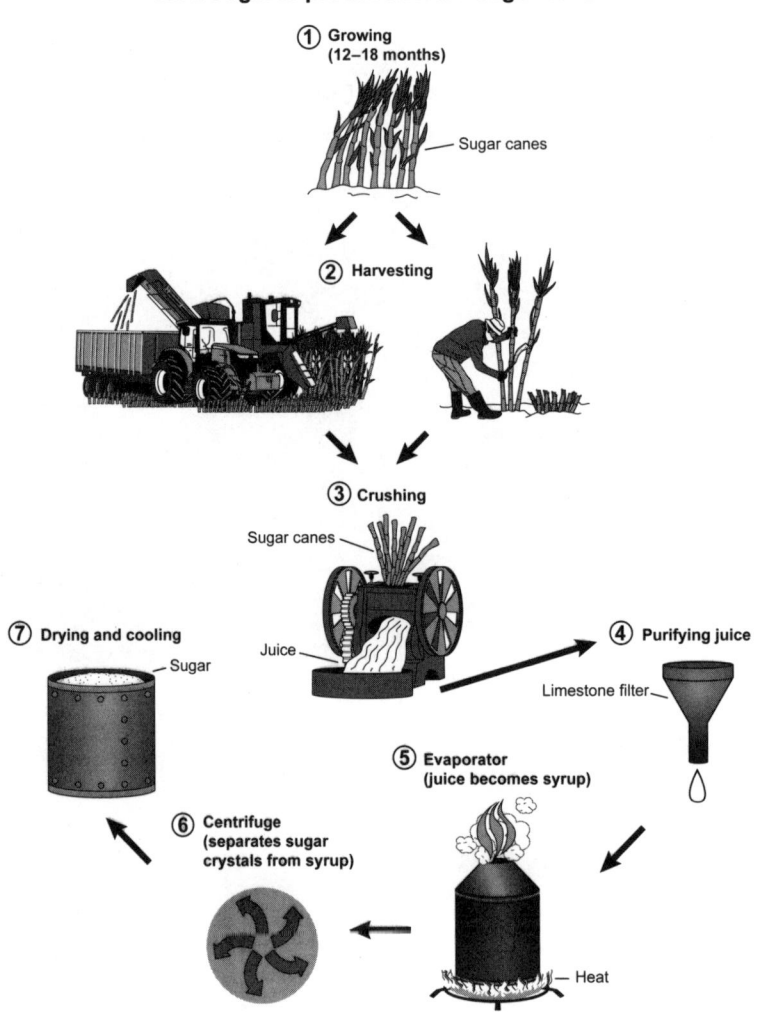

WRITING TASK 2

You should spend about 40 minutes on this task.

Write about the following topic:

> *In their advertising, businesses nowadays usually emphasise that their products are new in some way.*
>
> *Why is this? Do you think it is a positive or negative development?*

Give reasons for your answer and include any relevant examples from your own knowledge or experience.

Write at least 250 words.

PART 1

The examiner asks you about yourself, your home, work or studies and other familiar topics.

EXAMPLE

Flowers and plants

- Do you have a favourite flower or plant? [Why/Why not?]
- What kinds of flowers and plants grow near where you live? [Why/Why not?]
- Is it important to you to have flowers and plants in your home? [Why/Why not?]
- Have you ever bought flowers for someone else? [Why/Why not?]

PART 2

Describe a review you read about a product or service.

You should say:
   where you read the review
   what the product or service was
   what information the review gave about the product or service

and explain what you did as a result of reading this review.

You will have to talk about the topic for one to two minutes. You have one minute to think about what you are going to say. You can make some notes to help you if you wish.

PART 3

Discussion topics:

Online reviews

Example questions:
What kinds of things do people write online reviews about in your country?
Why do some people write online reviews?
Do you think that online reviews are good for both shoppers and companies?

Customer service

Example questions:
What do you think it might be like to work in a customer service job?
Do you agree that customers are more likely to complain nowadays?
How important is it for companies to take all customer complaints seriously?

Test 3

LISTENING

PART 1   *Questions 1–10*

Complete the notes below.

*Write **ONE WORD AND/OR A NUMBER** for each answer.*

Listening test audio

JUNIOR CYCLE CAMP

The course focuses on skills and safety.

- Charlie would be placed in Level 5.
- First of all, children at this level are taken to practise in a **1** ....

Instructors

- Instructors wear **2** .... shirts.
- A **3** .... is required and training is given.

Classes

- The size of the classes is limited.
- There are quiet times during the morning for a **4** .... or a game.
- Classes are held even if there is **5** ....

What to bring

- a change of clothing
- a **6** ....
- shoes (not sandals)
- Charlie's **7** ....

Day 1

- Charlie should arrive at 9.20 am on the first day.
- Before the class, his **8** .... will be checked.
- He should then go to the **9** .... to meet his class instructor.

Cost

- The course costs **10** $ .... per week.

PART 2   *Questions 11–20*

Questions 11 and 12

*Choose **TWO** letters, **A–E**.*

Listening test audio

According to Megan, what are the **TWO** main advantages of working in the agriculture and horticulture sectors?

    A   the active lifestyle
    B   the above-average salaries
    C   the flexible working opportunities
    D   the opportunities for overseas travel
    E   the chance to be in a natural environment

Questions 13 and 14

*Choose **TWO** letters, **A–E**.*

Which **TWO** of the following are likely to be disadvantages for people working outdoors?

    A   the increasing risk of accidents
    B   being in a very quiet location
    C   difficult weather conditions at times
    D   the cost of housing
    E   the level of physical fitness required

Questions 15–20

What information does Megan give about each of the following job opportunities?

*Choose **SIX** answers from the box and write the correct letter, **A–H**, next to Questions 15–20.*

Information

A   not a permanent job

B   involves leading a team

C   experience not essential

D   intensive work but also fun

E   chance to earn more through overtime

F   chance for rapid promotion

G   accommodation available

H   local travel involved

Job opportunities

15   Fresh food commercial manager   ....

16   Agronomist   ....

17   Fresh produce buyer   ....

18   Garden centre sales manager   ....

19   Tree technician   ....

20   Farm worker   ....

PART 3   *Questions 21–30*

Questions 21 and 22

Listening test audio

*Choose **TWO** letters, **A–E**.*

Which **TWO** points does Adam make about his experiment on artificial sweeteners?

   A   The results were what he had predicted.
   B   The experiment was simple to set up.
   C   A large sample of people was tested.
   D   The subjects were unaware of what they were drinking.
   E   The test was repeated several times for each person.

Questions 23 and 24

*Choose **TWO** letters, **A–E**.*

Which **TWO** problems did Rosie have when measuring the fat content of nuts?

   A   She used the wrong sort of nuts.
   B   She used an unsuitable chemical.
   C   She did not grind the nuts finely enough.
   D   The information on the nut package was incorrect.
   E   The weighing scales may have been unsuitable.

Questions 25–30

*Choose the correct letter, **A**, **B** or **C**.*

25 Adam suggests that restaurants could reduce obesity if their menus

    A   offered fewer options.
    B   had more low-calorie foods.
    C   were organised in a particular way.

26 The students agree that food manufacturers deliberately

    A   make calorie counts hard to understand.
    B   fail to provide accurate calorie counts.
    C   use ineffective methods to reduce calories.

27 What does Rosie say about levels of exercise in England?

    A   The amount recommended is much too low.
    B   Most people overestimate how much they do.
    C   Women now exercise more than they used to.

28 Adam refers to the location and width of stairs in a train station to illustrate

    A   practical changes that can influence people's behaviour.
    B   methods of helping people who have mobility problems.
    C   ways of preventing accidents by controlling crowd movement.

29 What do the students agree about including reference to exercise in their presentation?

    A   They should probably leave it out.
    B   They need to do more research on it.
    C   They should discuss this with their tutor.

30 What are the students going to do next for their presentation?

    A   prepare some slides for it
    B   find out how long they have for it
    C   decide on its content and organisation

PART 4   *Questions 31–40*

Complete the notes below.

*Write **ONE WORD ONLY** for each answer.*

Listening test audio

Hand knitting

Interest in knitting

- Knitting has a long history around the world.
- We imagine someone like a **31** .... knitting.
- A **32** .... ago, knitting was expected to disappear.
- The number of knitting classes is now increasing.
- People are buying more **33** .... for knitting nowadays.

Benefits of knitting

- gives support in times of **34** .... difficulty
- requires only **35** .... skills and little money to start
- reduces stress in a busy life

Early knitting

- The origins are not known.
- Findings show early knitted items to be **36** .... in shape.
- The first needles were made of natural materials such as wood and **37** ....
- Early yarns felt **38** .... to touch.
- Wool became the most popular yarn for spinning.
- Geographical areas had their own **39** .... of knitting.
- Everyday tasks like looking after **40** .... were done while knitting.

READING PASSAGE 1

*You should spend about 20 minutes on **Questions 1–13**, which are based on Reading Passage 1 below.*

Roman shipbuilding and navigation

Shipbuilding today is based on science and ships are built using computers and sophisticated tools. Shipbuilding in ancient Rome, however, was more of an art relying on estimation, inherited techniques and personal experience. The Romans were not traditionally sailors but mostly land-based people, who learned to build ships from the people that they conquered, namely the Greeks and the Egyptians.

There are a few surviving written documents that give descriptions and representations of ancient Roman ships, including the sails and rigging. Excavated vessels also provide some clues about ancient shipbuilding techniques. Studies of these have taught us that ancient Roman shipbuilders built the outer hull first, then proceeded with the frame and the rest of the ship. Planks used to build the outer hull were initially sewn together. Starting from the 6th century BCE, they were fixed using a method called mortise and tenon, whereby one plank locked into another without the need for stitching. Then in the first centuries of the current era, Mediterranean shipbuilders shifted to another shipbuilding method, still in use today, which consisted of building the frame first and then proceeding with the hull and the other components of the ship. This method was more systematic and dramatically shortened ship construction times. The ancient Romans built large merchant ships and warships whose size and technology were unequalled until the 16th century CE.

Warships were built to be lightweight and very speedy. They had to be able to sail near the coast, which is why they had no ballast or excess load and were built with a long, narrow hull. They did not sink when damaged and often would lie crippled on the sea's surface following naval battles. They had a bronze battering ram, which was used to pierce the timber hulls or break the oars of enemy vessels. Warships used both wind (sails) and human power (oarsmen) and were therefore very fast. Eventually, Rome's navy became the largest and most powerful in the Mediterranean, and the Romans had control over what they therefore called *Mare Nostrum* meaning 'our sea'.

There were many kinds of warship. The 'trireme' was the dominant warship from the 7th to 4th century BCE. It had rowers in the top, middle and lower levels, and approximately 50 rowers in each bank. The rowers at the bottom had the most uncomfortable position as they were under the other rowers and were exposed to the water entering through the oar-holes. It is worth noting that contrary to popular perception, rowers were not slaves but mostly Roman citizens enrolled in the military. The trireme was superseded by larger ships with even more rowers.

Merchant ships were built to transport lots of cargo over long distances and at a reasonable cost. They had a wider hull, double planking and a solid interior for added stability. Unlike warships, their V-shaped hull was deep underwater, meaning that they could not sail too close to the coast. They usually had two huge side rudders located off the stern and controlled by a small tiller bar connected to a system of cables. They had from one to three masts with large square sails and a small triangular sail at the bow. Just like warships, merchant ships used oarsmen, but coordinating the hundreds of rowers in both types of ship was not an easy task. In order to assist them, music would be played on an instrument, and oars would then keep time with this.

The cargo on merchant ships included raw materials (e.g. iron bars, copper, marble and granite), and agricultural products (e.g. grain from Egypt's Nile valley). During the Empire, Rome was a huge city by ancient standards of about one million inhabitants. Goods from all over the world would come to the city through the port of Pozzuoli situated west of the bay of Naples in Italy and through the gigantic port of Ostia situated at the mouth of the Tiber River. Large merchant ships would approach the destination port and, just like today, be intercepted by a number of towboats that would drag them to the quay.

The time of travel along the many sailing routes could vary widely. Navigation in ancient Rome did not rely on sophisticated instruments such as compasses but on experience, local knowledge and observation of natural phenomena. In conditions of good visibility, seamen in the Mediterranean often had the mainland or islands in sight, which greatly facilitated navigation. They sailed by noting their position relative to a succession of recognisable landmarks. When weather conditions were not good or where land was no longer visible, Roman mariners estimated directions from the pole star or, with less accuracy, from the Sun at noon. They also estimated directions relative to the wind and swell. Overall, shipping in ancient Roman times resembled shipping today with large vessels regularly crossing the seas and bringing supplies from their Empire.

Questions 1–5

Do the following statements agree with the information given in Reading Passage 1?

In boxes 1–5 on your answer sheet, write

> **TRUE**   *if the statement agrees with the information*
> **FALSE**   *if the statement contradicts the information*
> **NOT GIVEN**   *if there is no information on this*

1   The Romans' shipbuilding skills were passed on to the Greeks and the Egyptians.

2   Skilled craftsmen were needed for the mortise and tenon method of fixing planks.

3   The later practice used by Mediterranean shipbuilders involved building the hull before the frame.

4   The Romans called the Mediterranean Sea *Mare Nostrum* because they dominated its use.

5   Most rowers on ships were people from the Roman army.

Questions 6–13

Complete the summary below.

*Choose **ONE WORD ONLY** from the passage for each answer.*

Write your answers in boxes 6–13 on your answer sheet.

Warships and merchant ships

Warships were designed so that they were **6** .... and moved quickly. They often remained afloat after battles and were able to sail close to land as they lacked any additional weight. A battering ram made of **7** .... was included in the design for attacking and damaging the timber and oars of enemy ships. Warships, such as the 'trireme', had rowers on three different **8** ....

Unlike warships, merchant ships had a broad **9** .... that lay far below the surface of the sea. Merchant ships were steered through the water with the help of large rudders and a tiller bar. They had both square and **10** .... sails. On merchant ships and warships, **11** .... was used to ensure rowers moved their oars in and out of the water at the same time.

Quantities of agricultural goods such as **12** .... were transported by merchant ships to two main ports in Italy. The ships were pulled to the shore by **13** .... When the weather was clear and they could see islands or land, sailors used landmarks that they knew to help them navigate their route.

READING PASSAGE 2

*You should spend about 20 minutes on **Questions 14–26**, which are based on Reading Passage 2 below.*

Climate change reveals ancient artefacts in Norway's glaciers

A   Well above the treeline in Norway's highest mountains, ancient fields of ice are shrinking as Earth's climate warms. As the ice has vanished, it has been giving up the treasures it has preserved in cold storage for the last 6,000 years – items such as ancient arrows and skis from Viking Age* traders. And those artefacts have provided archaeologists with some surprising insights into how ancient Norwegians made their livings.

B   Organic materials like textiles and hides are relatively rare finds at archaeological sites. This is because unless they're protected from the microorganisms that cause decay, they tend not to last long. Extreme cold is one reliable way to keep artefacts relatively fresh for a few thousand years, but once thawed out, these materials experience degradation relatively swiftly.

    With climate change shrinking ice cover around the world, glacial archaeologists need to race the clock to find newly revealed artefacts, preserve them, and study them. If something fragile dries and is windblown it might very soon be lost to science, or an arrow might be exposed and then covered again by the next snow and remain well-preserved. The unpredictability means that glacial archaeologists have to be systematic in their approach to fieldwork.

C   Over a nine-year period, a team of archaeologists, which included Lars Pilø of Oppland County Council, Norway, and James Barrett of the McDonald Institute for Archaeological Research, surveyed patches of ice in Oppland, an area of south-central Norway that is home to some of the country's highest mountains. Reindeer once congregated on these icy patches in the later summer months to escape biting insects, and from the late Stone Age**, hunters followed. In addition, trade routes threaded through the mountain passes of Oppland, linking settlements in Norway to the rest of Europe.

    The slow but steady movement of glaciers tends to destroy anything at their bases, so the team focused on stationary patches of ice, mostly above 1,400 metres. That ice is found amid fields of frost-weathered boulders, fallen rocks, and exposed bedrock that for nine months of the year is buried beneath snow.

    'Fieldwork is hard work – hiking with all our equipment, often camping on permafrost – but very rewarding. You're rescuing the archaeology, bringing the melting ice to wider attention, discovering a unique environmental history and really connecting with the natural environment,' says Barrett.

---

*Viking Age: a period of European history from around 700 CE to around 1050 CE when Scandinavian Vikings migrated throughout Europe by means of trade and warfare

** The Stone Age: a period in early history that began about 3.4 million years ago

D   At the edges of the contracting ice patches, archaeologists found more than 2,000 artefacts, which formed a material record that ran from 4,000 BCE to the beginnings of the Renaissance in the 14th century. Many of the artefacts are associated with hunting. Hunters would have easily misplaced arrows and they often discarded broken bows rather than take them all the way home. Other items could have been used by hunters traversing the high mountain passes of Oppland: all-purpose items like tools, skis, and horse tack.

E   Barrett's team radiocarbon-dated 153 of the artefacts and compared those dates to the timing of major environmental changes in the region – such as periods of cooling or warming – and major social and economic shifts – such as the growth of farming settlements and the spread of international trade networks leading up to the Viking Age. They found that some periods had produced lots of artefacts, which indicates that people had been pretty active in the mountains during those times. But there were few or no signs of activity during other periods.

F   What was surprising, according to Barrett, was the timing of these periods. Oppland's mountains present daunting terrain and in periods of extreme cold, glaciers could block the higher mountain passes and make travel in the upper reaches of the mountains extremely difficult. Archaeologists assumed people would stick to lower elevations during a time like the Late Antique Little Ice Age, a short period of deeper-than-usual cold from about 536–600 CE. But it turned out that hunters kept regularly venturing into the mountains even when the climate turned cold, based on the amount of stuff they had apparently dropped there.

'Remarkably, though, the finds from the ice may have continued through this period, perhaps suggesting that the importance of mountain hunting increased to supplement failing agricultural harvests in times of low temperatures,' says Barrett. A colder turn in the Scandinavian climate would likely have meant widespread crop failures, so more people would have depended on hunting to make up for those losses.

G   Many of the artefacts Barrett's team recovered date from the beginning of the Viking Age, the 700s through to the 900s CE. Trade networks connecting Scandinavia with Europe and the Middle East were expanding around this time. Although we usually think of ships when we think of Scandinavian expansion, these recent discoveries show that plenty of goods travelled on overland routes, like the mountain passes of Oppland. And growing Norwegian towns, along with export markets, would have created a booming demand for hides to fight off the cold, as well as antlers to make useful things like combs. Business must have been good for hunters.

H   Norway's mountains are probably still hiding a lot of history – and prehistory – in remote ice patches. When Barrett's team looked at the dates for their sample of 153 artefacts, they noticed a gap with almost no artefacts from about 3,800 to 2,200 BCE. In fact, archaeological finds from that period are rare all over Norway. The researchers say that could be because many of those artefacts have already disintegrated or are still frozen in the ice. That means archaeologists could be extracting some of those artefacts from retreating ice in years to come.

Questions 14–19

Reading Passage 2 has eight sections, **A–H**.

Which section contains the following information?

*Write the correct letter, **A–H**, in boxes 14–19 on your answer sheet.*

14 an explanation for weapons being left behind in the mountains

15 a reference to the physical difficulties involved in an archaeological expedition

16 an explanation of why less food may have been available

17 a reference to the possibility of future archaeological discoveries

18 examples of items that would have been traded

19 a reference to the pressure archaeologists are under to work quickly

Questions 20–22

Complete the summary below.

*Choose **ONE WORD ONLY** from the passage for each answer.*

Write your answers in boxes 20–22 on your answer sheet.

Interesting finds at an archaeological site

Organic materials such as animal skins and textiles are not discovered very often at archaeological sites. They have little protection against **20** .... , which means that they decay relatively quickly. But this is not always the case. If temperatures are low enough, fragile artefacts can be preserved for thousands of years.

A team of archaeologists have been working in the mountains in Oppland in Norway to recover artefacts revealed by shrinking ice cover. In the past, there were trade routes through these mountains and **21** .... gathered there in the summer months to avoid being attacked by **22** .... on lower ground. The people who used these mountains left things behind and it is those objects that are of interest to archaeologists.

Questions 23 and 24

Choose **TWO** letters, **A–E**.

Write the correct letters in boxes 23 and 24 on your answer sheet.

Which **TWO** of the following statements does the writer make about the discoveries of Barrett's team?

    A   Artefacts found in the higher mountain passes were limited to skiing equipment.

    B   Hunters went into the mountains even during periods of extreme cold.

    C   The number of artefacts from certain time periods was relatively low.

    D   Radiocarbon dating of artefacts produced some unreliable results.

    E   More artefacts were found in Oppland than at any other mountain site.

Questions 25 and 26

Choose **TWO** letters, **A–E**.

Write the correct letters in boxes 25 and 26 on your answer sheet.

Which **TWO** of the following statements does the writer make about the Viking Age?

    A   Hunters at this time benefited from an increased demand for goods.

    B   The beginning of the period saw the greatest growth in the wealth of Vikings.

    C   Vikings did not rely on ships alone to transport goods.

    D   Norwegian towns at this time attracted traders from around the world.

    E   Vikings were primarily interested in their trading links with the Middle East.

READING PASSAGE 3

*You should spend about 20 minutes on **Questions 27–40**, which are based on Reading Passage 3 below.*

Plant 'thermometer' triggers springtime growth by measuring night-time heat

A photoreceptor molecule in plant cells has been found to have a second job as a thermometer after dark – allowing plants to read seasonal temperature changes. Scientists say the discovery could help breed crops that are more resilient to the temperatures expected to result from climate change

A   An international team of scientists led by the University of Cambridge has discovered that the 'thermometer' molecule in plants enables them to develop according to seasonal temperature changes. Researchers have revealed that molecules called phytochromes – used by plants to detect light during the day – actually change their function in darkness to become cellular temperature gauges that measure the heat of the night.

The new findings, published in the journal *Science*, show that phytochromes control genetic switches in response to temperature as well as light to dictate plant development.

B   At night, these molecules change states, and the pace at which they change is 'directly proportional to temperature', say scientists, who compare phytochromes to mercury in a thermometer. The warmer it is, the faster the molecular change – stimulating plant growth.

C   Farmers and gardeners have known for hundreds of years how responsive plants are to temperature: warm winters cause many trees and flowers to bud early, something humans have long used to predict weather and harvest times for the coming year. The latest research pinpoints for the first time a molecular mechanism in plants that reacts to temperature – often triggering the buds of spring we long to see at the end of winter.

D   With weather and temperatures set to become ever more unpredictable due to climate change, researchers say the discovery that this light-sensing molecule also functions as the internal thermometer in plant cells could help us breed tougher crops. 'It is estimated that agricultural yields will need to double by 2050, but climate change is a major threat to achieving this. Key crops such as wheat and rice are sensitive to high temperatures. Thermal stress reduces crop yields by around 10% for every one degree increase in temperature,' says lead researcher Dr Philip Wigge from Cambridge's Sainsbury Laboratory. 'Discovering the molecules that allow plants to sense temperature has the potential to accelerate the breeding of crops resilient to thermal stress and climate change.'

E In their active state, phytochrome molecules bind themselves to DNA to restrict plant growth. During the day, sunlight activates the molecules, slowing down growth. If a plant finds itself in shade, phytochromes are quickly inactivated – enabling it to grow faster to find sunlight again. This is how plants compete to escape each other's shade. 'Light-driven changes to phytochrome activity occur very fast, in less than a second,' says Wigge.

At night, however, it's a different story. Instead of a rapid deactivation following sundown, the molecules gradually change from their active to inactive state. This is called 'dark reversion'. 'Just as mercury rises in a thermometer, the rate at which phytochromes revert to their inactive state during the night is a direct measure of temperature,' says Wigge.

F 'The lower the temperature, the slower the rate at which phytochromes revert to inactivity, so the molecules spend more time in their active, growth-suppressing state. This is why plants are slower to grow in winter. Warm temperatures accelerate dark reversion, so that phytochromes rapidly reach an inactive state and detach themselves from the plant's DNA – allowing genes to be expressed and plant growth to resume.' Wigge believes phytochrome thermo-sensing evolved at a later stage, and co-opted the biological network already used for light-based growth during the downtime of night.

G Some plants mainly use day length as an indicator of the season. Other species, such as daffodils, have considerable temperature sensitivity, and can flower months in advance during a warm winter. In fact, the discovery of the dual role of phytochromes provides the science behind a well-known rhyme long used to predict the coming season: oak before ash we'll have a splash, ash before oak we're in for a soak.

Wigge explains: 'Oak trees rely much more on temperature, likely using phytochromes as thermometers to dictate development, whereas ash trees rely on measuring day length to determine their seasonal timing. A warmer spring, and consequently a higher likeliness of a hot summer, will result in oak leafing before ash. A cold spring will see the opposite. As the British know only too well, a colder summer is likely to be a rain-soaked one.'

H The new findings are the culmination of twelve years of research involving scientists from Germany, Argentina and the US, as well as the Cambridge team. The work was done in a model system, using a mustard plant called *Arabidopsis*, but Wigge says the phytochrome genes necessary for temperature sensing are found in crop plants as well. 'Recent advances in plant genetics now mean that scientists are able to rapidly identify the genes controlling these processes in crop plants, and even alter their activity using precise molecular "scalpels",' adds Wigge. 'Cambridge is uniquely well-positioned to do this kind of research as we have outstanding collaborators nearby who work on more applied aspects of plant biology, and can help us transfer this new knowledge into the field.'

Questions 27–32

Do the following statements agree with the information given in Reading Passage 3?

In boxes 27–32 on your answer sheet, write

> **TRUE**   *if the statement agrees with the information*
> **FALSE**   *if the statement contradicts the information*
> **NOT GIVEN** *if there is no information on this*

27 The Cambridge scientists' discovery of the 'thermometer molecule' caused surprise among other scientists.

28 The target for agricultural production by 2050 could be missed.

29 Wheat and rice suffer from a rise in temperatures.

30 It may be possible to develop crops that require less water.

31 Plants grow faster in sunlight than in shade.

32 Phytochromes change their state at the same speed day and night.

Questions 33–37

Reading Passage 3 has eight sections, **A–H**.

Which section contains the following information?

*Write the correct letter, **A–H**, in boxes 33–37 on your answer sheet.*

33 mention of specialists who can make use of the research findings

34 a reference to a potential benefit of the research findings

35 scientific support for a traditional saying

36 a reference to people traditionally making plans based on plant behaviour

37 a reference to where the research has been reported

Questions 38–40

Complete the sentences below.

*Choose **NO MORE THAN TWO WORDS** from the passage for each answer.*

Write your answers in boxes 38–40 on your answer sheet.

38 Daffodils are likely to flower early in response to .... weather.

39 If ash trees come into leaf before oak trees, the weather in ....
will probably be wet.

40 The research was carried out using a particular species of ....

WRITING

WRITING TASK 1

You should spend about 20 minutes on this task.

> *The plans below show the site of an airport now and how it will look after redevelopment next year.*
>
> *Summarise the information by selecting and reporting the main features, and make comparisons where relevant.*

Write at least 150 words.

SOUTHWEST AIRPORT

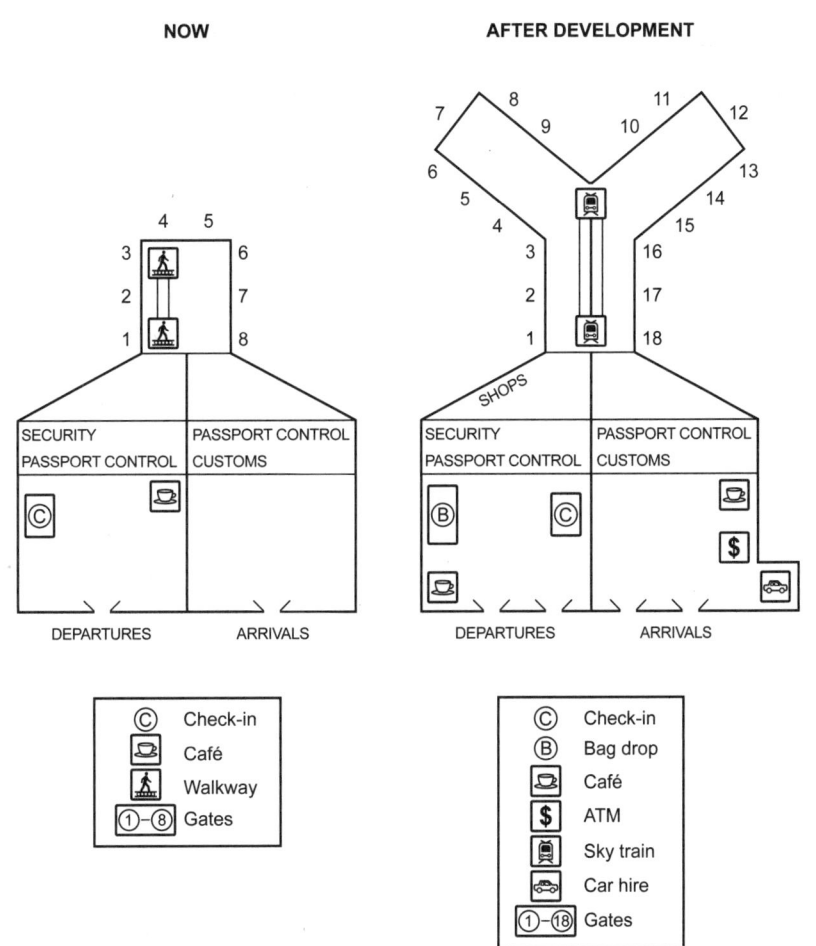

→ 📎 p. 135

WRITING TASK 2

You should spend about 40 minutes on this task.

Write about the following topic:

> *Many manufactured food and drink products contain high levels of sugar,*
> *which causes many health problems. Sugary products should be made more*
> *expensive to encourage people to consume less sugar.*
>
> *Do you agree or disagree?*

Give reasons for your answer and include any relevant examples from your own knowledge or experience.

Write at least 250 words.

SPEAKING

PART 1

The examiner asks you about yourself, your home, work or studies and other familiar topics.

EXAMPLE

Summer

- Is summer your favourite time of year? [Why/Why not?]
- What do you do in summer when the weather's very hot? [Why?]
- Do you go on holiday every summer? [Why/Why not?]
- Did you enjoy the summer holidays when you were at school? [Why/Why not?]

PART 2

Describe a luxury item you would like to own in the future.

You should say:
 what item you would like to own
 what this item looks like
 why you would like to own this item

and explain whether you think you will ever own this item.

You will have to talk about the topic for one to two minutes. You have one minute to think about what you are going to say. You can make some notes to help you if you wish.

PART 3

Discussion topics:

Expensive items

Example questions:
Which expensive items would many young people (in your country) like to buy?
How do the expensive items that younger people want to buy differ from those that older people want to buy?
Do you think that people are more likely to buy expensive items for their friends or for themselves?

Rich people

Example questions:
How difficult is it to become very rich in today's world?
Do you agree that money does not necessarily bring happiness?
In what ways might rich people use their money to help society?

Test 4

PART 1   *Questions 1–10*

Complete the notes below.

*Write **ONE WORD AND/OR A NUMBER** for each answer.*

Listening test audio

Holiday rental

Owners' names: Jack Fitzgerald and Shirley Fitzgerald

Granary Cottage
*   available for week beginning **1** .... May
*   cost for the week: **2** £ ....

3 .... **Cottage**
*   cost for the week: £480
*   building was originally a **4** ....
*   walk through doors from living room into a **5** ....
*   several **6** .... spaces at the front
*   bathroom has a shower
*   central heating and stove that burns **7** ....
*   views of old **8** .... from living room
*   view of hilltop **9** .... from the bedroom

Payment
*   deposit: £144
*   deadline for final payment: end of **10** ....

PART 2   *Questions 11–20*

Questions 11–14

*Choose the correct letter, **A**, **B** or **C**.*

Listening test audio

Local council report on traffic and highways

11 A survey found people's main concern about traffic in the area was

    A   cuts to public transport.
    B   poor maintenance of roads.
    C   changes in the type of traffic.

12 Which change will shortly be made to the cycle path next to the river?

    A   It will be widened.
    B   It will be extended.
    C   It will be resurfaced.

13 Plans for a pedestrian crossing have been postponed because

    A   the Post Office has moved.
    B   the proposed location is unsafe.
    C   funding is not available at present.

14 On Station Road, notices have been erected

    A   telling cyclists not to leave their bikes outside the station ticket office.
    B   asking motorists to switch off engines when waiting at the level crossing.
    C   warning pedestrians to leave enough time when crossing the railway line.

Questions 15–20

Label the map below.

*Write the correct letter, **A–I**, next to Questions 15–20.*

Recreation ground after proposed changes

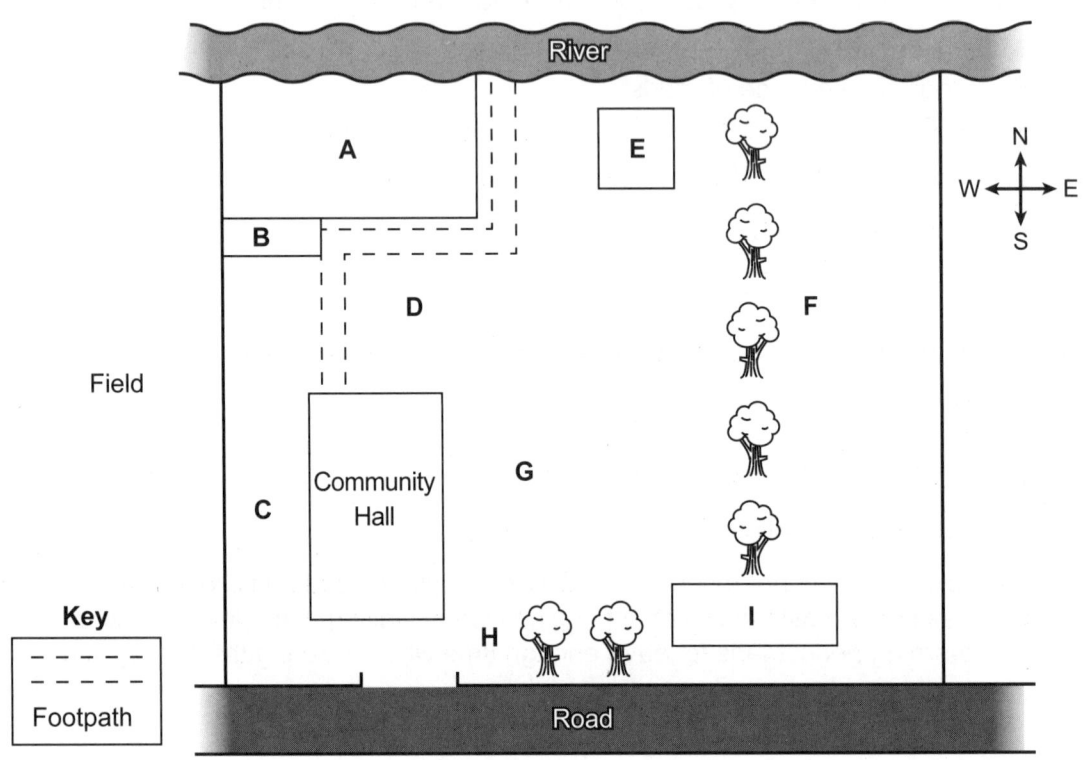

15	New car park	....
16	New cricket pitch	....
17	Children's playground	....
18	Skateboard ramp	....
19	Pavilion	....
20	Notice board	....

PART 3   *Questions 21–30*

Questions 21–22

*Choose **TWO** letters, **A–E**.*

Listening test audio

Which **TWO** benefits of city bike-sharing schemes do the students agree are the most important?

    A   reducing noise pollution
    B   reducing traffic congestion
    C   improving air quality
    D   encouraging health and fitness
    E   making cycling affordable

Questions 23–24

*Choose **TWO** letters, **A–E**.*

Which **TWO** things do the students think are necessary for successful bike-sharing schemes?

    A   Bikes should have a GPS system.
    B   The app should be easy to use.
    C   Public awareness should be raised.
    D   Only one scheme should be available.
    E   There should be a large network of cycle lanes.

Questions 25–30

What is the speakers' opinion of the bike-sharing schemes in each of the following cities?

*Choose **SIX** answers from the box and write the correct letter, **A–G**, next to Questions 25–30.*

Opinion of bike-sharing scheme

A   They agree it has been disappointing.

B   They think it should be cheaper.

C   They are surprised it has been so successful.

D   They agree that more investment is required.

E   They think the system has been well designed.

F   They disagree about the reasons for its success.

G   They think it has expanded too quickly.

Cities

25   Amsterdam   ....

26   Dublin   ....

27   London   ....

28   Buenos Aires   ....

29   New York   ....

30   Sydney   ....

PART 4   *Questions 31–40*

Complete the notes below.

*Write **ONE WORD ONLY** for each answer.*

Listening test audio

THE EXTINCTION OF THE DODO BIRD

The dodo was a large flightless bird which used to inhabit the island of Mauritius.

History

- 1507 – Portuguese ships transporting **31** .... stopped at the island to collect food and water.
- 1638 – The Dutch established a **32** .... on the island.
- They killed the dodo birds for their meat.
- The last one was killed in 1681.

Description

- The only record we have is written descriptions and pictures (possibly unreliable).
- A Dutch painting suggests the dodo was very **33** ....
- The only remaining soft tissue is a dried **34** ....
- Recent studies of a dodo skeleton suggest the birds were capable of rapid

  35 ....
- It's thought they were able to use their small wings to maintain

  36 ....
- Their **37** .... was of average size.
- Their sense of **38** .... enabled them to find food.

Reasons for extinction

- Hunting was probably not the main cause.
- Sailors brought dogs and monkeys.
- **39** .... also escaped onto the island and ate the birds' eggs.
- The arrival of farming meant the **40** .... was destroyed.

READING

READING PASSAGE 1

*You should spend about 20 minutes on **Questions 1–13**, which are based on Reading Passage 1 below.*

Roman tunnels

The Romans, who once controlled areas of Europe, North Africa and Asia Minor, adopted the construction techniques of other civilizations to build tunnels in their territories

The Persians, who lived in present-day Iran, were one of the first civilizations to build tunnels that provided a reliable supply of water to human settlements in dry areas. In the early first millennium BCE, they introduced the *qanat* method of tunnel construction, which consisted of placing posts over a hill in a straight line, to ensure that the tunnel kept to its route, and then digging vertical shafts down into the ground at regular intervals. Underground, workers removed the earth from between the ends of the shafts, creating a tunnel. The excavated soil was taken up to the surface using the shafts, which also provided ventilation during the work. Once the tunnel was completed, it allowed water to flow from the top of a hillside down towards a canal, which supplied water for human use. Remarkably, some *qanats* built by the Persians 2,700 years ago are still in use today.

They later passed on their knowledge to the Romans, who also used the *qanat* method to construct water-supply tunnels for agriculture. Roman *qanat* tunnels were constructed with vertical shafts dug at intervals of between 30 and 60 meters. The shafts were equipped with handholds and footholds to help those climbing in and out of them and were covered with a wooden or stone lid. To ensure that the shafts were vertical, Romans hung a plumb line from a rod placed across the top of each shaft and made sure that the weight at the end of it hung in the center of the shaft. Plumb lines were also used to measure the depth of the shaft and to determine the slope of the tunnel. The 5.6-kilometer-long Claudius tunnel, built in 41 CE to drain the Fucine Lake in central Italy, had shafts that were up to 122 meters deep, took 11 years to build and involved approximately 30,000 workers.

By the 6th century BCE, a second method of tunnel construction appeared called the *counter-excavation* method, in which the tunnel was constructed from both ends. It was used to cut through high mountains when the *qanat* method was not a practical alternative. This method required greater planning and advanced knowledge of surveying, mathematics and geometry as both ends of a tunnel had to meet correctly at the center of the mountain. Adjustments to the direction of the tunnel also had to be made whenever builders encountered geological problems or when it deviated from its set path. They constantly checked the tunnel's advancing direction, for example, by looking back at the light that penetrated through the tunnel mouth, and made corrections whenever necessary. Large deviations could happen, and they could result in one end of the tunnel not being usable. An inscription written on the side of a 428-meter tunnel, built by the Romans as part of the Saldae aqueduct system in modern-day Algeria, describes how the two teams of builders missed each other in the mountain and how the later construction of a lateral link between both corridors corrected the initial error.

The Romans dug tunnels for their roads using the counter-excavation method, whenever they encountered obstacles such as hills or mountains that were too high for roads to pass over. An example is the 37-meter-long, 6-meter-high, Furlo Pass Tunnel built in Italy in 69–79 CE. Remarkably, a modern road still uses this tunnel today. Tunnels were also built for mineral extraction. Miners would locate a mineral vein and then pursue it with shafts and tunnels underground. Traces of such tunnels used to mine gold can still be found at the Dolaucothi mines in Wales. When the sole purpose of a tunnel was mineral extraction, construction required less planning, as the tunnel route was determined by the mineral vein.

Roman tunnel projects were carefully planned and carried out. The length of time it took to construct a tunnel depended on the method being used and the type of rock being excavated. The *qanat* construction method was usually faster than the counter-excavation method as it was more straightforward. This was because the mountain could be excavated not only from the tunnel mouths but also from shafts. The type of rock could also influence construction times. When the rock was hard, the Romans employed a technique called fire quenching which consisted of heating the rock with fire, and then suddenly cooling it with cold water so that it would crack. Progress through hard rock could be very slow, and it was not uncommon for tunnels to take years, if not decades, to be built. Construction marks left on a Roman tunnel in Bologna show that the rate of advance through solid rock was 30 centimeters per day. In contrast, the rate of advance of the Claudius tunnel can be calculated at 1.4 meters per day. Most tunnels had inscriptions showing the names of patrons who ordered construction and sometimes the name of the architect. For example, the 1.4-kilometer Çevlik tunnel in Turkey, built to divert the floodwater threatening the harbor of the ancient city of Seleuceia Pieria, had inscriptions on the entrance, still visible today, that also indicate that the tunnel was started in 69 CE and was completed in 81 CE.

Questions 1–6

Label the diagrams below.

*Choose **ONE WORD ONLY** from the passage for each answer.*

Write your answers in boxes 1–6 on your answer sheet.

The Persian Qanat Method

1 .... to direct
the tunnelling

water runs into a 2 ....
used by local people

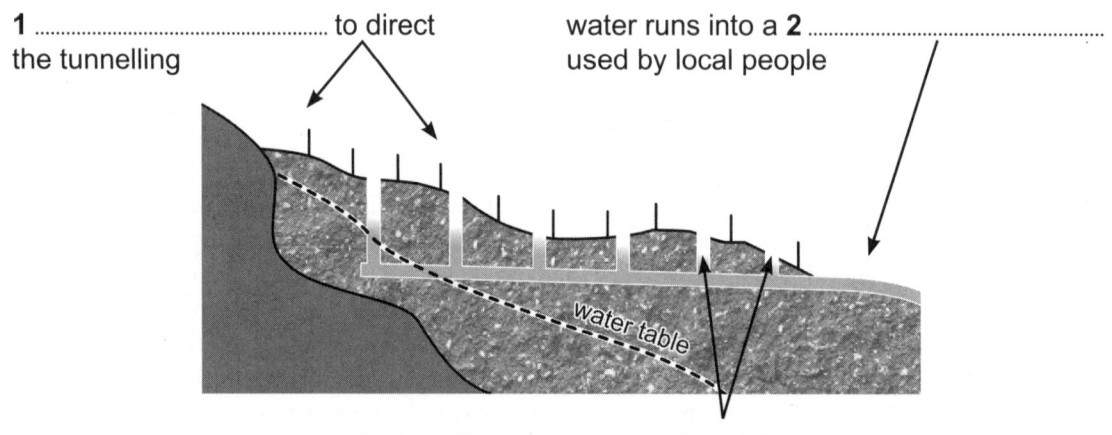

vertical shafts to remove earth and for 3 ....

Cross-section of a Roman Qanat Shaft

4 .... made of wood or stone

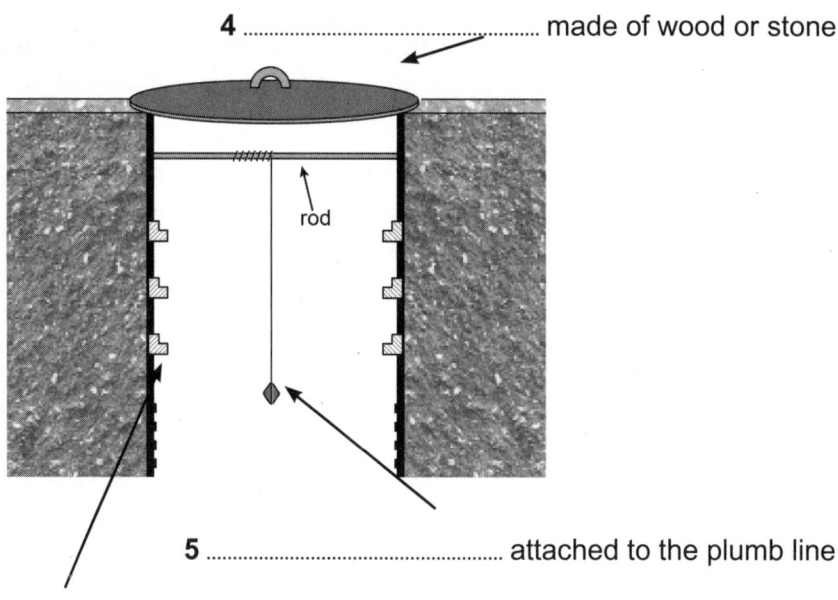

rod

5 .... attached to the plumb line

handholds and footholds used for 6 ....

Questions 7–10

Do the following statements agree with the information given in Reading Passage 1?

In boxes 7–10 on your answer sheet, write

> **TRUE**   *if the statement agrees with the information*
> **FALSE**   *if the statement contradicts the information*
> **NOT GIVEN**   *if there is no information on this*

7   The counter-excavation method completely replaced the qanat method in the 6th century BCE.

8   Only experienced builders were employed to construct a tunnel using the counter-excavation method.

9   The information about a problem that occurred during the construction of the Saldae aqueduct system was found in an ancient book.

10   The mistake made by the builders of the Saldae aqueduct system was that the two parts of the tunnel failed to meet.

Questions 11–13

Answer the questions below.

Choose **NO MORE THAN TWO WORDS** *from the passage for each answer.*

Write your answers in boxes 11–13 on your answer sheet.

11   What type of mineral were the Dolaucothi mines in Wales built to extract?

12   In addition to the patron, whose name might be carved onto a tunnel?

13   What part of Seleuceia Pieria was the Çevlik tunnel built to protect?

READING PASSAGE 2

*You should spend about 20 minutes on **Questions 14–26**, which are based on Reading Passage 2 below.*

Changes in reading habits

What are the implications of the way we read today?

Look around on your next plane trip. The iPad is the new pacifier for babies and toddlers. Younger school-aged children read stories on smartphones; older kids don't read at all, but hunch over video games. Parents and other passengers read on tablets or skim a flotilla of email and news feeds. Unbeknown to most of us, an invisible, game-changing transformation links everyone in this picture: the neuronal circuit that underlies the brain's ability to read is subtly, rapidly changing and this has implications for everyone from the pre-reading toddler to the expert adult.

As work in neurosciences indicates, the acquisition of literacy necessitated a new circuit in our species' brain more than 6,000 years ago. That circuit evolved from a very simple mechanism for decoding basic information, like the number of goats in one's herd, to the present, highly elaborated reading brain. My research depicts how the present reading brain enables the development of some of our most important intellectual and affective processes: internalized knowledge, analogical reasoning, and inference; perspective-taking and empathy; critical analysis and the generation of insight. Research surfacing in many parts of the world now cautions that each of these essential 'deep reading' processes may be under threat as we move into digital-based modes of reading.

This is not a simple, binary issue of print versus digital reading and technological innovation. As MIT scholar Sherry Turkle has written, we do not err as a society when we innovate but when we ignore what we disrupt or diminish while innovating. In this hinge moment between print and digital cultures, society needs to confront what is diminishing in the expert reading circuit, what our children and older students are not developing, and what we can do about it.

We know from research that the reading circuit is not given to human beings through a genetic blueprint like vision or language; it needs an environment to develop. Further, it will adapt to that environment's requirements – from different writing systems to the characteristics of whatever medium is used. If the dominant medium advantages processes that are fast, multi-task oriented and well-suited for large volumes of information, like the current digital medium, so will the reading circuit. As UCLA psychologist Patricia Greenfield writes, the result is that less attention and time will be allocated to slower, time-demanding deep reading processes.

Increasing reports from educators and from researchers in psychology and the humanities bear this out. English literature scholar and teacher Mark Edmundson describes how many college students actively avoid the classic literature of the 19th and 20th centuries in favour of something simpler as they no longer have the patience to read longer, denser, more difficult texts. We should be less concerned with students' 'cognitive impatience', however, than by what may underlie it: the potential inability of large numbers of students to read with a level of critical analysis sufficient to comprehend the complexity of thought and argument found in more demanding texts.

Multiple studies show that digital screen use may be causing a variety of troubling downstream effects on reading comprehension in older high school and college students. In Stavanger, Norway, psychologist Anne Mangen and her colleagues studied how high school students comprehend the same material in different mediums. Mangen's group asked subjects questions about a short story whose plot had universal student appeal; half of the students read the story on a tablet, the other half in paperback. Results indicated that students who read on print were superior in their comprehension to screen-reading peers, particularly in their ability to sequence detail and reconstruct the plot in chronological order.

Ziming Liu from San Jose State University has conducted a series of studies which indicate that the 'new norm' in reading is skimming, involving word-spotting and browsing through the text. Many readers now use a pattern when reading in which they sample the first line and then word-spot through the rest of the text. When the reading brain skims like this, it reduces time allocated to deep reading processes. In other words, we don't have time to grasp complexity, to understand another's feelings, to perceive beauty, and to create thoughts of the reader's own.

The possibility that critical analysis, empathy and other deep reading processes could become the unintended 'collateral damage' of our digital culture is not a straightforward binary issue about print versus digital reading. It is about how we all have begun to read on various mediums and how that changes not only what we read, but also the purposes for which we read. Nor is it only about the young. The subtle atrophy of critical analysis and empathy affects us all equally. It affects our ability to navigate a constant bombardment of information. It incentivizes a retreat to the most familiar stores of unchecked information, which require and receive no analysis, leaving us susceptible to false information and irrational ideas.

There's an old rule in neuroscience that does not alter with age: use it or lose it. It is a very hopeful principle when applied to critical thought in the reading brain because it implies choice. The story of the changing reading brain is hardly finished. We possess both the science and the technology to identify and redress the changes in how we read before they become entrenched. If we work to understand exactly what we will lose, alongside the extraordinary new capacities that the digital world has brought us, there is as much reason for excitement as caution.

Questions 14–17

*Choose the correct letter, **A**, **B**, **C** or **D**.*

Write the correct letter in boxes 14–17 on your answer sheet.

14   What is the writer's main point in the first paragraph?

   A   Our use of technology is having a hidden effect on us.
   B   Technology can be used to help youngsters to read.
   C   Travellers should be encouraged to use technology on planes.
   D   Playing games is a more popular use of technology than reading.

15   What main point does Sherry Turkle make about innovation?

   A   Technological innovation has led to a reduction in print reading.
   B   We should pay attention to what might be lost when innovation occurs.
   C   We should encourage more young people to become involved in innovation.
   D   There is a difference between developing products and developing ideas.

16   What point is the writer making in the fourth paragraph?

   A   Humans have an inborn ability to read and write.
   B   Reading can be done using many different mediums.
   C   Writing systems make unexpected demands on the brain.
   D   Some brain circuits adjust to whatever is required of them.

17   According to Mark Edmundson, the attitude of college students

   A   has changed the way he teaches.
   B   has influenced what they select to read.
   C   does not worry him as much as it does others.
   D   does not match the views of the general public.

Questions 18–22

*Complete the summary using the list of words, **A–H**, below.*

*Write the correct letter, **A–H**, in boxes 18–22 on your answer sheet.*

Studies on digital screen use

There have been many studies on digital screen use, showing some **18** .... trends. Psychologist Anne Mangen gave high-school students a short story to read, half using digital and half using print mediums. Her team then used a question-and-answer technique to find out how **19** .... each group's understanding of the plot was. The findings showed a clear pattern in the responses, with those who read screens finding the order of information **20** .... to recall.

Studies by Ziming Liu show that students are tending to read **21** .... words and phrases in a text to save time. This approach, she says, gives the reader a superficial understanding of the **22** .... content of material, leaving no time for thought.

A fast	**B** isolated	**C** emotional	**D** worrying
E many	**F** hard	**G** combined	**H** thorough

Questions 23–26

Do the following statements agree with the views of the writer in Reading Passage 2?

In boxes 23–26 on your answer sheet, write

> **YES** — *if the statement agrees with the views of the writer*
> **NO** — *if the statement contradicts the views of the writer*
> **NOT GIVEN** — *if it is impossible to say what the writer thinks about this*

23 The medium we use to read can affect our choice of reading content.

24 Some age groups are more likely to lose their complex reading skills than others.

25 False information has become more widespread in today's digital era.

26 We still have opportunities to rectify the problems that technology is presenting.

READING PASSAGE 3

*You should spend about 20 minutes on **Questions 27–40**, which are based on Reading Passage 3 on pages 91 and 92.*

Questions 27–32

Reading Passage 3 has six sections, **A–F**.

Choose the correct heading for each section from the list of headings below.

*Write the correct number, **i–viii**, in boxes 27–32 on your answer sheet.*

List of Headings

i	An increasing divergence of attitudes towards AI
ii	Reasons why we have more faith in human judgement than in AI
iii	The superiority of AI projections over those made by humans
iv	The process by which AI can help us make good decisions
v	The advantages of involving users in AI processes
vi	Widespread distrust of an AI innovation
vii	Encouraging openness about how AI functions
viii	A surprisingly successful AI application

---

27 Section **A**

28 Section **B**

29 Section **C**

30 Section **D**

31 Section **E**

32 Section **F**

Attitudes towards Artificial Intelligence

A   Artificial intelligence (AI) can already predict the future. Police forces are using it to map when and where crime is likely to occur. Doctors can use it to predict when a patient is most likely to have a heart attack or stroke. Researchers are even trying to give AI imagination so it can plan for unexpected consequences.

Many decisions in our lives require a good forecast, and AI is almost always better at forecasting than we are. Yet for all these technological advances, we still seem to deeply lack confidence in AI predictions. Recent cases show that people don't like relying on AI and prefer to trust human experts, even if these experts are wrong.

If we want AI to really benefit people, we need to find a way to get people to trust it. To do that, we need to understand why people are so reluctant to trust AI in the first place.

B   Take the case of Watson for Oncology, one of technology giant IBM's supercomputer programs. Their attempt to promote this program to cancer doctors was a PR disaster. The AI promised to deliver top-quality recommendations on the treatment of 12 cancers that accounted for 80% of the world's cases. But when doctors first interacted with Watson, they found themselves in a rather difficult situation. On the one hand, if Watson provided guidance about a treatment that coincided with their own opinions, physicians did not see much point in Watson's recommendations. The supercomputer was simply telling them what they already knew, and these recommendations did not change the actual treatment.

On the other hand, if Watson generated a recommendation that contradicted the experts' opinion, doctors would typically conclude that Watson wasn't competent. And the machine wouldn't be able to explain why its treatment was plausible because its machine-learning algorithms were simply too complex to be fully understood by humans. Consequently, this has caused even more suspicion and disbelief, leading many doctors to ignore the seemingly outlandish AI recommendations and stick to their own expertise.

C   This is just one example of people's lack of confidence in AI and their reluctance to accept what AI has to offer. Trust in other people is often based on our understanding of how others think and having experience of their reliability. This helps create a psychological feeling of safety. AI, on the other hand, is still fairly new and unfamiliar to most people. Even if it can be technically explained (and that's not always the case), AI's decision-making process is usually too difficult for most people to comprehend. And interacting with something we don't understand can cause anxiety and give us a sense that we're losing control.

Many people are also simply not familiar with many instances of AI actually working, because it often happens in the background. Instead, they are acutely aware of instances where AI goes wrong. Embarrassing AI failures receive a disproportionate amount of media attention, emphasising the message that we cannot rely on technology. Machine learning is not foolproof, in part because the humans who design it aren't.

D Feelings about AI run deep. In a recent experiment, people from a range of backgrounds were given various sci-fi films about AI to watch and then asked questions about automation in everyday life. It was found that, regardless of whether the film they watched depicted AI in a positive or negative light, simply watching a cinematic vision of our technological future polarised the participants' attitudes. Optimists became more extreme in their enthusiasm for AI and sceptics became even more guarded.

This suggests people use relevant evidence about AI in a biased manner to support their existing attitudes, a deep-rooted human tendency known as "confirmation bias". As AI is represented more and more in media and entertainment, it could lead to a society split between those who benefit from AI and those who reject it. More pertinently, refusing to accept the advantages offered by AI could place a large group of people at a serious disadvantage.

E Fortunately, we already have some ideas about how to improve trust in AI. Simply having previous experience with AI can significantly improve people's opinions about the technology, as was found in the study mentioned above. Evidence also suggests the more you use other technologies such as the internet, the more you trust them.

Another solution may be to reveal more about the algorithms which AI uses and the purposes they serve. Several high-profile social media companies and online marketplaces already release transparency reports about government requests and surveillance disclosures. A similar practice for AI could help people have a better understanding of the way algorithmic decisions are made.

F Research suggests that allowing people some control over AI decision-making could also improve trust and enable AI to learn from human experience. For example, one study showed that when people were allowed the freedom to slightly modify an algorithm, they felt more satisfied with its decisions, more likely to believe it was superior and more likely to use it in the future.

We don't need to understand the intricate inner workings of AI systems, but if people are given a degree of responsibility for how they are implemented, they will be more willing to accept AI into their lives.

Questions 33–35

*Choose the correct letter, **A**, **B**, **C** or **D**.*

Write the correct letter in boxes 33–35 on your answer sheet.

33 What is the writer doing in Section A?

    A   providing a solution to a concern
    B   justifying an opinion about an issue
    C   highlighting the existence of a problem
    D   explaining the reasons for a phenomenon

34 According to Section C, why might some people be reluctant to accept AI?

    A   They are afraid it will replace humans in decision-making jobs.
    B   Its complexity makes them feel that they are at a disadvantage.
    C   They would rather wait for the technology to be tested over a period of time.
    D   Misunderstandings about how it works make it seem more challenging than it is.

35 What does the writer say about the media in Section C of the text?

    A   It leads the public to be mistrustful of AI.
    B   It devotes an excessive amount of attention to AI.
    C   Its reports of incidents involving AI are often inaccurate.
    D   It gives the impression that AI failures are due to designer error.

Questions 36–40

Do the following statements agree with the claims of the writer in Reading Passage 3?

In boxes 36–40 on your answer sheet, write

> **YES**   *if the statement agrees with the claims of the writer*
> **NO**   *if the statement contradicts the claims of the writer*
> **NOT GIVEN**   *if it is impossible to say what the writer thinks about this*

36 Subjective depictions of AI in sci-fi films make people change their opinions about automation.

37 Portrayals of AI in media and entertainment are likely to become more positive.

38 Rejection of the possibilities of AI may have a negative effect on many people's lives.

39 Familiarity with AI has very little impact on people's attitudes to the technology.

40 AI applications which users are able to modify are more likely to gain consumer approval.

WRITING

WRITING TASK 1

You should spend about 20 minutes on this task.

The diagram below shows the process for recycling plastic bottles.

Summarise the information by selecting and reporting the main features, and make comparisons where relevant.

Write at least 150 words.

How plastic bottles are recycled

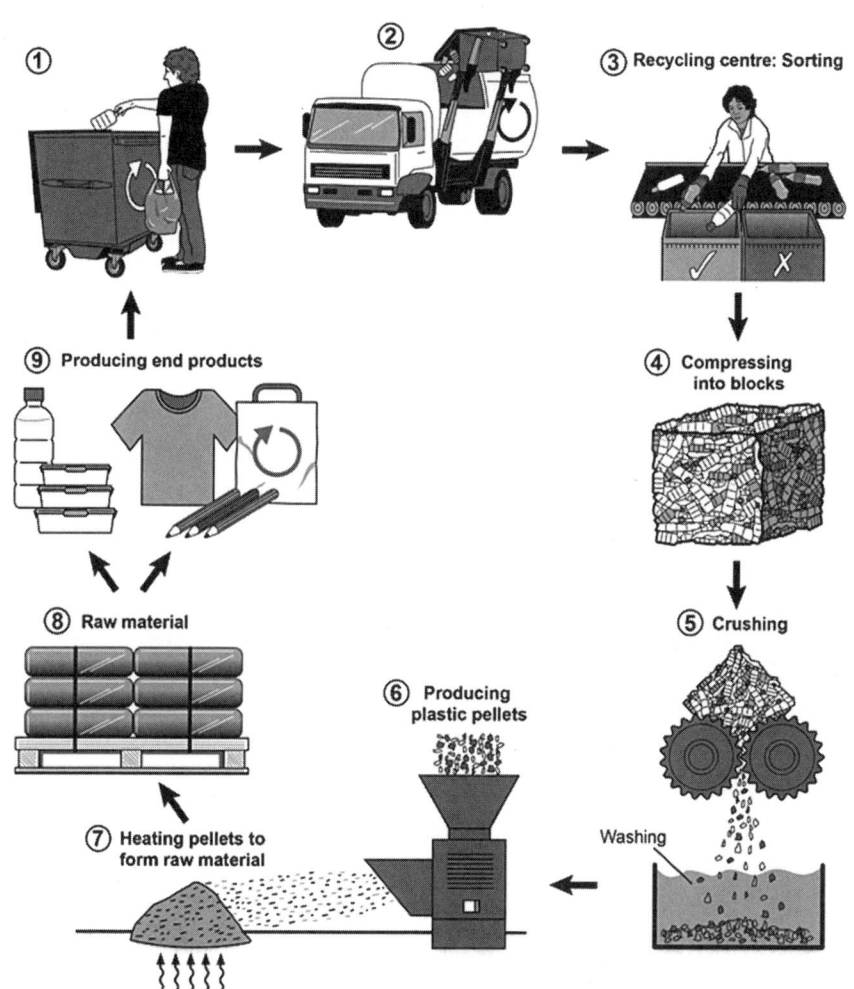

→ 🖉 p. 137

WRITING TASK 2

You should spend about 40 minutes on this task.

Write about the following topic:

In the future all cars, buses and trucks will be driverless. The only people travelling inside these vehicles will be passengers.

Do you think the advantages of driverless vehicles outweigh the disadvantages?

Give reasons for your answer and include any relevant examples from your own knowledge or experience.

Write at least 250 words.

SPEAKING

PART 1

The examiner asks you about yourself, your home, work or studies and other familiar topics.

EXAMPLE

Fast food

- What kinds of fast food have you tried? [Why/Why not?]
- Do you ever use a microwave to cook food quickly? [Why/Why not?]
- How popular are fast food restaurants where you live? [Why/Why not?]
- When would you go to a fast-food restaurant? [Why/Why not?]

PART 2

> **Describe some technology (e.g. an app, phone, software program) that you decided to stop using.**
>
> **You should say:**
>> **when and where you got this technology**
>> **why you started using this technology**
>> **why you decided to stop using it**
>
> **and explain how you feel about the decision you made.**

You will have to talk about the topic for one to two minutes. You have one minute to think about what you are going to say. You can make some notes to help you if you wish.

PART 3

Discussion topics:

Computer games

Example questions:
What kinds of computer games do people play in your country?
Why do people enjoy playing computer games?
Do you think that all computer games should have a minimum age for players?

Technology in the classroom

Example questions:
In what ways can technology in the classroom be helpful?
Do you agree that students are often better at using technology than their teachers?
Do you believe that computers will ever replace human teachers?

Audioscripts

TEST 1

PART 1

SARAH:	Hello. Children's Engineering Workshops.
FATHER:	Oh hello. I wanted some information about the workshops in the school holidays.
SARAH:	Sure.
FATHER:	I have two daughters who are interested. The younger one's Lydia, she's four – do you take children as young as that?
SARAH:	Yes, our Tiny Engineers workshop is for four to five-year-olds.
FATHER:	What sorts of activities do they do?
SARAH:	All sorts. For example, they work together to design a special cover that goes round an <u>egg</u>, so that when it's inside they can drop it from a height and it doesn't break. Well, sometimes it does break but that's part of the fun!
FATHER:	Right. And Lydia loves building things. Is there any opportunity for her to do that?
SARAH:	Well, they have a competition to see who can make the highest <u>tower</u>. You'd be amazed how high they can go.
FATHER:	Right.
SARAH:	But they're learning all the time as well as having fun. For example, one thing they do is to design and build a <u>car</u> that's attached to a balloon, and the force of the air in that actually powers the car and makes it move along. They go really fast too.
SARAH:	OK, well, all this sounds perfect.

Q1
Q2
Q3

FATHER:	Now Carly, that's my older daughter, has just had her seventh birthday, so presumably she'd be in a different group?
SARAH:	Yes, she'd be in the Junior Engineers. That's for children from six to eight.
FATHER:	And do they do the same sorts of activities?
SARAH:	Some are the same, but a bit more advanced. So they work out how to build model vehicles, things like cars and trucks, but also how to construct <u>animals</u> using the same sorts of material and technique, and then they learn how they can program them and make them move.
FATHER:	So they learn a bit of coding?
SARAH:	They do. They pick it up really quickly. We're there to help if they need it, but they learn from one another too.
FATHER:	Right. And do they have competitions too?
SARAH:	Yes, with the Junior Engineers, it's to use recycled materials like card and wood to build a <u>bridge</u>, and the longest one gets a prize.
FATHER:	That sounds fun. I wouldn't mind doing that myself!
SARAH:	Then they have something a bit different, which is to think up an idea for a five-minute <u>movie</u> and then film it, using special animation software. You'd be amazed what they come up with.
FATHER:	And of course, that's something they can put on their phone and take home to show all their friends.
SARAH:	Exactly. And then they also build a robot in the shape of a human, and they <u>decorate</u> it and program it so that it can move its arms and legs.

Q4
Q5
Q6
Q7

FATHER:	Perfect. So, is it the same price as the Tiny Engineers?
SARAH:	It's just a bit more: £50 for the five weeks.
FATHER:	And are the classes on a Monday, too?
SARAH:	They used to be, but we found it didn't give our staff enough time to clear up after the first workshop, so we moved them to <u>Wednesdays</u>. The classes are held in the morning from ten to eleven.
FATHER:	OK. That's better for me actually. And what about the location? Where exactly are the workshops held?
SARAH:	They're in building 10A – there's a big sign on the door, you can't miss it, and that's in <u>Fradstone</u> Industrial Estate.
FATHER:	Sorry?
SARAH:	Fradstone – that's F-R-A-D-S-T-O-N-E.
FATHER:	And that's in Grasford, isn't it?
SARAH:	Yes, up past the station.
FATHER:	And will I have any <u>parking</u> problems there?
SARAH:	No, there's always plenty available. So would you like to enrol Lydia and Carly now?
FATHER:	OK.
SARAH:	So can I have your full name …

Q8

Q9

Q10

PART 2

Good morning, everyone, and welcome to Stevenson's, one of the country's major manufacturers of metal goods. Thank you for choosing us for your two weeks of work experience. My name is Julia Simmons, and since the beginning of this year I've been the managing director.

Stevenson's is quite an old company. Like me, the founder, Ronald Stevenson, went into the steel industry when he left school – that was in 1923. <u>He set up this company when he finished his apprenticeship, in 1926</u>, although he actually started making plans two years earlier, in 1924. He was a very determined young man!

Q11

Stevenson's long-term plan was to manufacture components for the machine tools industry – although in fact that never came about – and for the automotive industry, that is, cars and lorries. However, there was a delay of five years before that happened, because shortly before the company went into production, <u>Stevenson was given the opportunity to make goods for hospitals and other players in the healthcare industry, so that's what we did for the first five years</u>.

Q12

Over the years, we've expanded the premises considerably – we were lucky that the site is big enough, so <u>moving to a new location has never been necessary</u>. However, the layout is far from ideal for modern machinery and production methods, so <u>we intend to carry out major refurbishment of this site</u> over the next five years.

Q13

I'd better give you some idea of what you'll be doing during your two weeks with us, so you know what to expect. <u>Most mornings you'll have a presentation from one of the managers</u>, to learn about their department, starting this morning with research and development. And you'll all spend some time in each department, observing what's going on and talking to people – as long as you don't stop them from doing their work altogether! In the past, a teacher from your school has come in at the end of each week to find out how the group were getting on, but your school isn't able to arrange that this year.

Q14

OK, now I'll briefly help you to orientate yourselves around the site. As you can see, we're in the reception area, which we try to make attractive and welcoming to visitors. There's a corridor running left from here, and <u>if you go along that, the door facing you at the end is the entrance to the coffee room. This looks out onto the main road on one side, and some trees on the other</u>, and that'll be where you meet each morning.   Q15

The factory is the very big room on the far side of the site. Next to it is <u>the warehouse, which can be accessed by lorries going up the road to the turning area at the end. You can get to the warehouse by crossing to the far side of the courtyard, and then the door is on your right</u>.   Q16

Somewhere you'll be keen to find is <u>the staff canteen. This is right next to reception</u>. I can confidently say that the food's very good, but the view isn't. <u>The windows on one side look onto a corridor and courtyard</u>, which aren't very attractive at all, <u>and on the other onto the access road</u>, which isn't much better.   Q17

You'll be using <u>the meeting room</u> quite often, and <u>you'll find it by walking along the corridor to the left of the courtyard, and continuing along it to the end. The meeting room is the last one on the right</u>, and I'm afraid <u>there's no natural daylight in the room</u>.   Q18

Then you'll need to know where some of the offices are. <u>The human resources department is at the front of this building, so you head to the left along the corridor from reception, and it's the second room you come to. It looks out onto the main road</u>.   Q19

And finally, <u>the boardroom</u>, where you'll be meeting sometimes. That has quite a pleasant view, as it <u>looks out on to the trees. Go along the corridor past the courtyard, right to the end. The boardroom is on the left, next to the factory</u>.   Q20

OK, now are there any questions before we …

PART 3

JESS:	How are you getting on with your art project, Tom?
TOM:	OK. Like, they gave us the theme of birds to base our project on, and I'm not really all that interested in wildlife. But I'm starting to get into it. I've pretty well finished the introductory stage.
JESS:	So have I. When they gave us <u>all those handouts with details of books and websites to look at</u>, I was really put off, but <u>the more I read, the more interested I got</u>.
TOM:	<u>Me too. I found I could research so many different aspects of birds in art – colour, movement, texture.</u> So I was looking forward to the Bird Park visit.
JESS:	What a letdown! It poured with rain and we hardly saw a single bird. <u>Much less use than the trip to the Natural History Museum</u>.
TOM:	<u>Yeah.</u> <u>I liked all the stuff about evolution there.</u> The workshop sessions with Dr Fletcher were good too, especially the brainstorming sessions.
JESS:	I missed those because I was ill. I wish we could've seen the projects last year's students did.
TOM:	Mm. I suppose they want us to do our own thing, not copy.
JESS:	Have you drafted your proposal yet?
TOM:	Yes, but I haven't handed it in. I need to amend some parts. I've realised the notes from my research are almost all just descriptions, <u>I haven't actually evaluated anything. So I'll have to fix that.</u>
JESS:	Oh, I didn't know we had to do that. <u>I'll have to look at that too.</u> Did you do a timeline for the project?
TOM:	Yes, and a mind map.
JESS:	Yeah, so did I. I quite enjoyed that. But it was hard having to explain the basis for my decisions in my action plan.

Q21/Q22 (next to "all those handouts...the more interested I got")

Q21/Q22 (next to "Much less use than the trip to the Natural History Museum")

Q23/Q24 (next to "I haven't actually evaluated anything. So I'll have to fix that.")

TOM:	What?
JESS:	You know, give a rationale.
TOM:	I didn't realise we had to do that. OK, I can add it now. And I've done the video diary presentation, and worked out what I want my outcome to be in the project.
JESS:	Someone told me it's best not to be too precise about your actual outcome at this stage, so you have more scope to explore your ideas later on. So I'm going to go back to my proposal to make it a bit more vague.
TOM:	Really? OK, I'll change that too then.

Q23/Q24

TOM:	One part of the project I'm unsure about is where we choose some paintings of birds and say what they mean to us. Like, I chose a painting of a falcon by Landseer. I like it because the bird's standing there with his head turned to one side, but he seems to be staring straight at you. But I can't just say it's a bit scary, can I?
JESS:	You could talk about the possible danger suggested by the bird's look.
TOM:	Oh, OK.
JESS:	There's a picture of a fish hawk by Audubon I like. It's swooping over the water with a fish in its talons, and with great black wings which take up most of the picture.
TOM:	So you could discuss it in relation to predators and food chains?
JESS:	Well actually I think I'll concentrate on the impression of rapid motion it gives.
TOM:	Right.
JESS:	Do you know that picture of a kingfisher by van Gogh – it's perching on a reed growing near a stream.
TOM:	Yes it's got these beautiful blue and red and black shades.
JESS:	Mm hm. I've actually chosen it because I saw a real kingfisher once when I was little, I was out walking with my grandfather, and I've never forgotten it.
TOM:	So we can use a personal link?
JESS:	Sure.
TOM:	OK. There's a portrait called *William Wells*, I can't remember the artist but it's a middle-aged man who's just shot a bird. And his expression, and the way he's holding the bird in his hand suggests he's not sure about what he's done. To me it's about how ambiguous people are in the way they exploit the natural world.
JESS:	Interesting. There's Gauguin's picture *Vairumati*. He did it in Tahiti. It's a woman with a white bird behind her that is eating a lizard, and what I'm interested in is what idea this bird refers to. Apparently, it's a reference to the never-ending cycle of existence.
TOM:	Wow. I chose a portrait of a little boy, Giovanni de Medici. He's holding a tiny bird in one fist. I like the way he's holding it carefully so he doesn't hurt it.
JESS:	Ah right.

Q25 (at "You could talk about the possible danger...")
Q26 (at "I'll concentrate on the impression of rapid motion")
Q27 (at "I saw a real kingfisher once when I was little")
Q28 (at "it's about how ambiguous people are...")
Q29 (at "it's a reference to the never-ending cycle")
Q30 (at "a portrait of a little boy, Giovanni de Medici")

PART 4

Ancient philosophy is not just about talking or lecturing, or even reading long, dense books. In fact, it is something people have used throughout history – to solve their problems and to achieve their greatest triumphs.

Specifically, I am referring to Stoicism, which, in my opinion, is the most practical of all philosophies and therefore the most appealing. Stoicism was founded in Ancient Greece by Zeno of Citium in the early 3rd century BC, but was practised by the likes of Epictetus, Cato,

Q31

Seneca and Marcus Aurelius. Amazingly, we still have access to these ideas, despite the fact that <u>the most famous Stoics never wrote anything down for publication</u>. Cato definitely didn't. Marcus Aurelius never intended his *Meditations* to be anything but personal. Seneca's letters were, well, letters and Epictetus' thoughts come to us by way of a note-taking student. **Q32**

Stoic principles were based on the idea that its followers could have an unshakable happiness in this life and the key to achieving this was virtue. The road to virtue, in turn, lay in understanding that destructive emotions, like anger and jealousy, are under our conscious control – they don't have to control us, because we can learn to control them. In the words of Epictetus: <u>"external events I cannot control, but the choices I make with regard to them, I do control"</u>. **Q33**

The modern day philosopher and writer Nassim Nicholas Taleb defines a Stoic as someone who has <u>a different perspective on experiences which most of us would see as wholly negative</u>; a Stoic "transforms fear into caution, pain into transformation, mistakes into initiation and desire into undertaking". Using this definition as a model, we can see that throughout the centuries Stoicism has been practised in more recent history by kings, presidents, artists, writers and entrepreneurs. **Q34**

The founding fathers of the United States were inspired by the philosophy. George Washington was introduced to Stoicism by his neighbours at age seventeen, and later, <u>put on a play based on the life of Cato to inspire his men</u>. Thomas Jefferson kept a copy of Seneca beside his bed. **Q35**

Writers and artists have also been inspired by the stoics. Eugène Delacroix, the renowned French Romantic artist (known best for his painting *Liberty Leading the People*) was an ardent Stoic, referring to it as his "consoling religion".

The economist <u>Adam Smith's theories on capitalism were significantly influenced by the Stoicism</u> that he studied as a schoolboy, under a teacher who had translated Marcus Aurelius' works. **Q36**

Today's political leaders are no different, with many finding their inspiration from the ancient texts. Former US president Bill Clinton rereads Marcus Aurelius every single year, and many have compared former President Obama's calm leadership style to that of Cato. Wen Jiabao, the former prime minister of China, claims that *Meditations* is one of two books he travels with and that he has read it more than one hundred times over the course of his life.

Stoicism had a profound influence on Albert Ellis, who invented <u>Cognitive Behaviour Therapy</u>, which is used to help people manage their problems by changing the way that they think and behave. <u>It's most commonly used to treat depression.</u> The idea is that we can take control of our lives by <u>challenging the irrational beliefs that create our faulty thinking, symptoms and behaviours by using logic</u> instead. **Q37** **Q38**

Stoicism has also become popular in the world of business. Stoic principles can build the resilience and state of mind required to overcome setbacks because <u>Stoics teach turning obstacles into opportunity</u>. A lesson every business entrepreneur needs to learn. **Q39**

I would argue that studying Stoicism is as relevant today as it was 2,000 years ago, thanks to its brilliant <u>insights into how to lead a good life</u>. At the very root of the thinking, there is a very **Q40** simple way of living – control what you can and accept what you can't. <u>This is not as easy as it sounds and will require considerable practice</u> – it can take a lifetime to master. The Stoics also believed the most important foundation for a good and happy life is not money, fame, power or pleasure, but having a disciplined and principled character – something which seems to resonate with many people today.

PART 1

EMPLOYEE:	Hello, Picturercp. Can I help you?
WOMAN:	Oh, hi. I saw your advertisement about copying pictures to disk and I'd like a bit more information about what you do.
EMPLOYEE:	Sure. What would you like to know?
WOMAN:	Well, I've got a box full of old family photos that's been up in the attic for years, some of them must be 50 or 60 years old, and I'd like to get them converted to digital format.
EMPLOYEE:	Sure, we can do that for you.
WOMAN:	Right. And what about size? The photos are all sorts of sizes – are there any restrictions?
EMPLOYEE:	Well the maximum size of photo we can do with our normal service is 30 centimetres. And each picture must be at least 4 centimetres, that's the minimum we can cope with.
WOMAN:	That should be fine. And some of them are in a <u>frame</u> – should I take them out before I send them?
EMPLOYEE:	Yes please, we can't copy them otherwise. And also the photos must all be separate, they mustn't be stuck into an album.
WOMAN:	OK, that's not a problem. So can you give me an idea of how much this will cost? I've got about 360 photos I think.
EMPLOYEE:	We charge <u>£195 for 300 to 400 photos</u> for the basic service.
WOMAN:	OK. And does that include the disk?
EMPLOYEE:	Yes, one disk – but you can get extra ones for £5 each.
WOMAN:	That's good. So do I need to pay when I send you the photos?
EMPLOYEE:	No, we won't need anything until we've actually copied the pictures. Then we'll let you know how much it is, and <u>once we've received the payment</u>, we'll send the parcel off to you.
WOMAN:	Right.

Q1

Q2

Q3

EMPLOYEE:	Is there anything else you'd like to ask about our services?
WOMAN:	Yes. I've roughly sorted out the photos into groups, according to what they're about – so can you keep them in those groups when you copy them.
EMPLOYEE:	Sure. We'll save each group in a different folder on the disk and if you like, you can suggest a name for each folder –
WOMAN:	So I could have one called <u>'Grandparents'</u> for instance?
EMPLOYEE:	Exactly.
WOMAN:	And do you do anything besides scan the photos? Like, can you make any improvements?
EMPLOYEE:	Yes, in the standard service each photo is checked, and we can sometimes <u>touch up the colour</u> a bit, or improve the contrast – that can make a big difference.
WOMAN:	OK. And some of the photos are actually quite fragile – they won't get damaged in the process, will they?
EMPLOYEE:	No, if any look particularly fragile, <u>we'd do them by hand</u>. We do realise how precious these old photos can be.
WOMAN:	Sure.
EMPLOYEE:	And another thing is we can make changes to a photo if you want – so if you want to remove an object from a photo, or maybe <u>alter the background</u>, we can do that.

Q4

Q5

Q6

Q7

104

WOMAN:	Really? I might be interested in that. I'll have a look through the photos and see. Oh, and talking of fixing photos – I've got a few <u>that aren't properly in focus</u>. Can you do anything to make that better?	*Q8*
EMPLOYEE:	No, I'm afraid that's one thing we can't do.	
WOMAN:	OK.	
EMPLOYEE:	Any other information I can give you?	
WOMAN:	Er … oh, how long will it all take?	
EMPLOYEE:	We aim to get the copying done <u>in ten days</u>.	*Q9*
WOMAN:	Fine. Right, well I'll get the photos packed up in a box and post them off to you.	
EMPLOYEE:	Right. If you've got a strong cardboard box, that's best. We've found that <u>plastic ones sometimes break in the post</u>.	*Q10*
WOMAN:	OK. Right, thanks for your help. Bye.	
EMPLOYEE:	Bye.	

PART 2

Good morning and thank you for coming here today. I'd like to bring you up to date with changes in the school that will affect your children.

As you know, the school buildings date from various times: some from the 1970s, some from the last five years, and of course Dartfield House is over a century old. It was commissioned by a businessman, Neville Richards, and intended as his family home, but he died before it was completed. <u>His heir chose to sell it to the local council, who turned it into offices.</u> A later plan to convert it into a tourist information centre didn't come about, through lack of money, and instead it formed the nucleus of this school when it opened 40 years ago.   *Q11*

The school has grown as the local population has increased, and I can now give you some news about the lower school site, which is separated from the main site by a road. Planning permission has been granted for development of both sites. The lower school will move to new buildings that will be constructed on the main site. <u>Developers will construct houses on the existing lower school site.</u> Work on the new school buildings should start within the next few months.   *Q12*

A more imminent change concerns the catering facilities and the canteen. The canteen is always very busy throughout the lunch period – in fact it's often full to capacity, because a lot of our pupils like the food that's on offer there. But there's only one serving point, so <u>most pupils have to wait a considerable time to be served</u>. This is obviously unsatisfactory, as they may have hardly finished their lunch before afternoon lessons start.   *Q13*

So we've had a new Food Hall built, and this will come into use next week. It'll have several serving areas, and I'll give you more details about those in a minute, but one thing we ask you to do, to help in the smooth running of the Food Hall, is to <u>discuss with your children each morning which type of food they want to eat that day</u>, so they can go straight to the relevant serving point. There won't be any junk food – everything on offer will be healthy – and there's no change to the current system of paying for lunches by topping up your child's electronic payment card online.   *Q14*

You may be wondering what will happen to the old canteen. <u>We'll still have tables and chairs in there, and pupils can eat food from the Food Hall or lunch they've brought from home.</u> Eventually we may use part of the canteen for storage, but first we'll see how many pupils go in there at lunchtime.   *Q15*

OK, back to the serving points in the Food Hall, which will all have side dishes, desserts and drinks on sale, as well as main courses.

One serving point we call <u>World Adventures</u>. This will serve <u>a different country's cuisine each</u>   *Q16*
<u>day</u>, maybe Chinese one day and Lebanese the next. The menus will be planned for a week at a time, so pupils will know what's going to be available the whole of that week.

<u>Street Life</u> is also international, with food from three particular cultures. <u>We'll ask pupils</u>   *Q17*
<u>to make suggestions</u>, so perhaps sometimes there'll be food from Thailand, Ethiopia and Mexico, and then one of them will be replaced by Jamaican food for a week or two.

The <u>Speedy Italian</u> serving point <u>will cater particularly for the many pupils who don't eat meat</u>   *Q18*
<u>or fish</u>: they can be sure that all the food served there is suitable for them. There'll be plenty of variety, so they shouldn't get bored with the food.

OK, that's all on the new Food Hall. Now after-school lessons. These are very popular with pupils, particularly swimming – in fact there's a waiting list for lessons. Cycling is another favourite, and I'm delighted that dozens of pupils make use of the chance to learn to ride in off-road conditions. It means that more and more cycle to and from school every day. As you know, we have a well-equipped performance centre, and <u>we're going to start drama classes</u>   *Q19/Q20*
in there, too. Pupils will be able to join in just for fun or work up to taking part in a play – we hope to put on at least one a year. We already teach a number of pupils to use the sound and lighting systems in the centre. And a former pupil has given a magnificent grand <u>piano</u> to the school, so <u>a few pupils will be able to learn at the school instead of going to the local college</u>,   *Q19/Q20*
as many of them do at the moment.

PART 3

SUSIE: So Luke, for our next psychology assignment we have to do something on sleep and dreams.

LUKE: Right. I've just read an article suggesting why we tend to forget most of our dreams soon after we wake up. I mean, most of my dreams aren't that interesting anyway, but what it said was that if we remembered everything, <u>we might get</u>   *Q21*
<u>mixed up about what actually happened and what we dreamed</u>. So it's a sort of protection. I hadn't heard that idea before. I'd always assumed that it was just that we didn't have room in our memories for all that stuff.

SUSIE: Me too. What do you think about the idea that our dreams may predict the future?

LUKE: It's a belief that you get all over the world.

SUSIE: Yeah, lots of people have a story of it happening to them, but the explanation I've read is that <u>for each dream that comes true, we have thousands that don't</u>,   *Q22*
but we don't notice those, we don't even remember them. We just remember the ones where something in the real world, like a view or an action, happens to trigger a dream memory.

LUKE: Right. So <u>it's just a coincidence really</u>. Something else I read about is what they call segmented sleeping. That's a theory that hundreds of years ago, people used to get up in the middle of the night and have a chat or something to eat, then go back to bed. So I tried it myself.

SUSIE: Why?

LUKE: Well it's meant to make you more creative. I don't know why. But I gave it up after a week. It just didn't fit in with my lifestyle.

SUSIE:	But most pre-school children have a short sleep in the day don't they? There was an experiment some students did here last term to see at what age kids should stop having naps. But <u>they didn't really find an answer</u>. They spent a lot of time working out the most appropriate methodology, but <u>the results didn't seem to show any obvious patterns</u>.	*Q23*
LUKE:	Right. Anyway, let's think about our assignment. Last time <u>I had problems with the final stage, where we had to describe and justify how successful we thought we'd been</u>. I struggled a bit with the action plan too.	*Q24*
SUSIE:	I was OK with the planning, but <u>I got marked down for the self-assessment as well</u>. And I had big problems with the statistical stuff, that's where I really lost marks.	
LUKE:	Right.	

SUSIE:	So shall we plan what we have to do for this assignment?	
LUKE:	OK.	
SUSIE:	First, we have to decide on our research question. So how about 'Is there a relationship between hours of sleep and number of dreams?'	
LUKE:	OK. Then we need to think about who we'll do the study on. About 12 people?	
SUSIE:	Right. And shall we use other psychology students?	
LUKE:	<u>Let's use people from a different department. What about history?</u>	*Q25*
SUSIE:	<u>Yes</u>, they might have interesting dreams! Or literature students?	
LUKE:	I don't really know any.	
SUSIE:	OK, forget that idea. Then we have to think about our methodology. So we could use observation, but that doesn't seem appropriate.	
LUKE:	No. It needs to be self-reporting I think. And we could ask them to answer questions online.	
SUSIE:	But in this case, <u>paper might be better</u> as they'll be doing it straight after they wake up … in fact while they're still half-asleep.	*Q26*
LUKE:	<u>Right.</u> And we'll have to <u>check the ethical guidelines</u> for this sort of research.	*Q27*
SUSIE:	Mm, <u>because our experiment involves humans,</u> so <u>there are special regulations</u>.	
LUKE:	Yes, I had a look at those for another assignment I did. There's a whole section on risk assessment, and another section on <u>making sure they aren't put under any unnecessary stress</u>.	*Q28*
SUSIE:	Let's hope they don't have any bad dreams!	
LUKE:	Yeah.	
SUSIE:	Then when we've collected all our data we have to analyse it and calculate the correlation between our two variables, that's time sleeping and number of dreams and then <u>present our results visually in a graph</u>.	*Q29*
LUKE:	Right. And the final thing is to think about <u>our research</u> and <u>evaluate it</u>. So that seems quite straightforward.	*Q30*
SUSIE:	Yeah. So now let's …	

PART 4

Dancing is something that humans do when they want to have a good time. It's a universal response to music, found in all cultures. But what's only been discovered recently is that dancing not only makes us feel good, it's also extremely good for our health.

Dancing, like other forms of exercise, releases hormones, such as dopamine, which make us feel relaxed and happy. And it also reduces feelings of stress or anxiety.

Dancing is also a sociable activity, which is another reason it makes us feel good.

One study compared people's enjoyment of dancing at home in front of a video with dancing in a group in a studio.

The people dancing in a group reported feeling happier, whereas those dancing alone did not.

In another experiment, university researchers at York and Sheffield took a group of students and sent each of them into a lab where music was played for five minutes. Each had to choose from three options: to sit and listen quietly to the music, to cycle on an exercise bike while they listened, or to get up and dance. All were given cognitive tasks to perform before and after. The result showed that those who chose to dance showed much more creativity   *Q31* when doing problem-solving tasks.

Doctor Lovatt at the University of Hertfordshire believes dance could be a very useful way to help people suffering from mental health problems. He thinks dance should be prescribed as   *Q32* therapy to help people overcome issues such as depression.

It's well established that dance is a good way of encouraging adolescent girls to take exercise but what about older people? Studies have shown that there are enormous benefits for people in their sixties and beyond. One of the great things about dance is that there are no barriers to participation. Anyone can have a go, even those whose standard of fitness is   *Q33* quite low.

Dance can be especially beneficial for older adults who can't run or do more intense workouts, or for those who don't want to. One 2015 study found that even a gentle dance workout helps to promote a healthy heart. And there's plenty of evidence which suggests that dancing lowers the risk of falls, which could result in a broken hip, for example, by helping people to improve their balance.   *Q34*

There are some less obvious benefits of dance for older people too. One thing I hadn't realised before researching this topic was that dance isn't just a physical challenge. It also requires a lot of concentration because you need to remember different steps and routines. For older people, this kind of activity is especially important because it forces their brain to   *Q35* process things more quickly and to retain more information.

Current research also shows that dance promotes a general sense of well-being in older participants, which can last up to a week after a class. Participants report feeling less tired and having greater motivation to be more active and do daily activities such as gardening or   *Q36* walking to the shops or a park.

Ballroom or country dancing, both popular with older people, have to be done in groups. They require collaboration and often involve touching a dance partner, all of which encourages interaction on the dance floor. This helps to develop new relationships and can reduce older   *Q37* people's sense of isolation, which is a huge problem in many countries.

I also looked at the benefits of Zumba. Fifteen million people in 180 countries now regularly take a Zumba class, an aerobic workout based on Latin American dance moves. John Porcari, a professor of exercise and sport science at the University of Wisconsin, analysed a group of women who were Zumba regulars and found that a class lasting 40 minutes burns   *Q38* about 370 calories. This is similar to moderately intense exercises like step aerobics or kickboxing.

A study in the *American Journal of Health Behavior* showed that when women with obesity did Zumba three times a week for 16 weeks, they lost an average of 1.2 kilos and lowered their percentage of body fat by 1%. More importantly, the women enjoyed the class so much that they made it a habit and continued to attend classes at least once a week – very unusual for an aerobic exercise programme.

Dance is never going to compete with high-intensity workouts when it comes to physical fitness gains, but its popularity is likely to keep on rising because it's such a fun way to keep fit.

Q39

Q40

PART 1

JAKE:	Hello, Junior Cycle camp, Jake speaking.
WOMAN:	Hi. I'm calling for some information about the cycle camp – I'm thinking of sending my son.
JAKE:	Great. Well, it's held every weekday morning over the summer vacation and we focus on basic cycling skills and safety. We have eight levels for children from three years upwards. How old's your son?
WOMAN:	Charlie? He's seven. He can ride a bike, but he needs a little more training before he's safe to go on the road.
JAKE:	He'd probably be best in Level 5. They start off practising on the site here, and we aim to get them riding on the road, but <u>first they're taken to ride in the park</u>, away from the traffic.
WOMAN:	Right. And can you tell me a bit about the instructors?
JAKE:	Well, all our staff wear different coloured shirts. So, we have three supervisors, and they have red shirts. They support the instructors, and they also stand in for me if I'm not around. Then <u>the instructors themselves are in blue shirts</u>, and one of these is responsible for each class.
WOMAN:	OK.
JAKE:	In order to be accepted, all our instructors <u>have to submit a reference</u> from someone who's seen them work with children – like if they've worked as a babysitter, for example. Then they have to complete our training course, including how to do lesson plans, and generally care for the well-being of the kids in their class. They do a great job, I have to say.
WOMAN:	Right. And tell me a bit about the classes. What size will Charlie's class be?
JAKE:	We have a limit of eight children in each class, so their instructor really gets to know them well. They're out riding most of the time but they have <u>quiet times too, where their instructor might tell them a story</u> that's got something to do with cycling, or get them to play a game together. It's a lot of fun.
WOMAN:	It must be. Now, <u>what happens if there's rain? Do the classes still run?</u>
JAKE:	<u>Oh yes.</u> We don't let that put us off – we just put on our waterproofs and keep cycling.

Q1

Q2

Q3

Q4

Q5

WOMAN:	And is there anything special Charlie should bring along with him?
JAKE:	Well, maybe some spare clothes, especially if the weather's not so good. And <u>a snack</u> for break time.
WOMAN:	How about a drink?
JAKE:	No, we'll provide that. And make sure he has shoes, not sandals.
WOMAN:	Sure. And just at present <u>Charlie has to take medication every few hours, so I'll make sure he has that</u>.
JAKE:	Absolutely. Just give us details of when he has to take it and we'll make sure he does.
WOMAN:	Thanks.
JAKE:	Now, there are a few things you should know about Day 1 of the camp. The classes normally start at 9.30 every morning, but on Day 1 you should aim to get Charlie here by 9.20. The finishing time will be 12.30 as usual. We need the additional time because there are a few extra things to do. The most important is that we have a very careful <u>check to make sure that every child's helmet fits</u>

Q6

Q7

Q8

properly. If it doesn't fit, we'll try to adjust it, or we'll find him another one – but he
must wear it all the time he's on the bike.

WOMAN: Of course.

JAKE: Then after that, all the instructors will be waiting to meet their classes, and <u>they'll</u>   Q9
           <u>meet up in the tent</u> – you can't miss it. And each instructor will take their class
           away and get started.

WOMAN: OK. Well that all sounds good. Now can you tell me how much the camp costs a
           week?

JAKE: <u>One hundred ninety-nine dollars.</u> We've managed to keep the price more or less   Q10
           the same as last year – it was one hundred ninety then. But the places are filling
           up quite quickly.

WOMAN: Right. OK, well I'd like to book for …

PART 2

Hello everyone. My name's Megan Baker and I'm a recruitment consultant at AVT
Recruitment specialists.

Now, our company specialises in positions that involve working in the agriculture and
horticulture sectors, so that's fresh food production, garden and park maintenance and so on.
And these sectors do provide some very special career opportunities. For a start, they often
offer <u>opportunities for those who don't want to be stuck with a 40-hour week, but need to</u>   Q11/Q12
<u>juggle work with other responsibilities</u> such as child care – and this is very important for many
of our recruits. Some people like working in a rural setting, surrounded by plants and trees
instead of buildings, although we can't guarantee that. But there are <u>certainly health benefits,</u>   Q11/Q12
<u>especially in jobs where you're not sitting all day looking at a screen</u> – a big plus for many
people. Salaries can sometimes be good too, although there's a lot of variety here. And you
may have the opportunity in some types of jobs for travel overseas, although that obviously
depends on the job, and not everyone is keen to do it.

Of course, working outdoors does have its challenges. It's fine in summer, but <u>can be</u>   Q13/Q14
<u>extremely unpleasant when it's cold and windy.</u> You may need to be pretty fit for some jobs,
though with modern technology that's not as important as it once was. And standards of
health and safety are much higher now than they used to be, so there are fewer work-related
accidents. But <u>if you like a lively city environment surrounded by lots of people, these jobs</u>   Q13/Q14
<u>are probably not for you – they're often in pretty remote areas.</u> And some people worry about
finding a suitable place to live, but in our experience, this usually turns out fine.

Now let me tell you about some of the exciting jobs that we have on our books right now.

One is for a <u>fresh food commercial manager.</u> Our client here is a very large fresh food
producer supplying a range of top supermarkets. They operate in a <u>very fast-paced</u>   Q15
<u>environment</u> with low profit margins – the staff there <u>work hard, but they play hard as well</u>, so
if you've a sociable personality this may be for you.

We have an exciting post as an <u>agronomist</u> advising farmers on issues such as crop nutrition,
protection against pests, and the latest legislation on farming and agricultural practices. There
are <u>good opportunities for the right person to quickly make their way up the career ladder</u>, but   Q16
a deep knowledge of the agricultural sector is expected of applicants.

A leading supermarket is looking for a <u>fresh produce buyer</u> who is available for a <u>12-month</u>   Q17
<u>maternity cover</u> contract. You need to have experience in administration, planning and buying
in the fresh produce industry, and in return will receive a very competitive salary.

We have also received a request for a <u>sales manager for a chain of garden centres</u>. You will <u>be visiting centres in the region</u> to ensure their high levels of customer service are maintained. This post is only suitable for someone who is prepared to live in the region. *Q18*

There is also a vacancy for a <u>tree technician</u> to carry out tree cutting, forestry and conservation work. Candidates must have a clean driving licence and have training in safety procedures. A year's experience would be preferred but <u>the company might be prepared to consider someone who has just completed an appropriate training course</u>. *Q19*

Finally, we have a position for a <u>farm worker</u>. This will involve a wide range of farm duties including crop sowing and harvesting, machine maintenance and animal care. Perks of the job include <u>the possibility of renting a small cottage on the estate</u>, and the chance to earn a competitive salary. A driving licence and tractor driving experience are essential. *Q20*

PART 3

ADAM: OK Rosie, shall we try to get some ideas together for our presentation on diet and obesity?

ROSIE: Sure.

ADAM: I can talk about the experiment I did to see if people can tell the difference between real sugar and artificial sweeteners.

ROSIE: Where you gave people drinks with either sugar or artificial sweeteners and they had to say which they thought it was?

ADAM: Yeah. It took me ages to decide exactly how I'd organise it, especially how I could make sure that <u>people didn't know which drink I was giving them</u>. It was hard to keep track of it all, especially as <u>I had so many people doing it</u> – I had to make sure I kept a proper record of what each person had had. *Q21/Q22* *Q21/Q22*

ROSIE: So could most people tell the difference?

ADAM: Yeah – I hadn't thought they would be able to, but most people could.

ROSIE: Then there's that experiment I did measuring the fat content of nuts, to see if the nutritional information given on the packet was accurate.

ADAM: The one where you ground up the nuts and mixed them with a chemical to absorb the fat?

ROSIE: Yes. My results were a bit problematic – the fat content for that type of nut seemed much lower than it said on the package. But I reckon the package information was right. I think <u>I should probably have ground up the nuts more than I did</u>. <u>It's possible that the scales for weighing the fat weren't accurate enough</u>, too. I'd really like to try the experiment again some time. *Q23/Q24* *Q23/Q24*

ADAM: So what can we say about helping people to lose weight?
There's a lot we could say about what restaurants could do to reduce obesity. I read that the items at the start of a menu and the items at the end of a menu are much more likely to be chosen than the items in the middle. So, <u>if you put the low-calorie items at the beginning and end of the menu, people will probably go for the food with fewer calories</u>, without even realising what they're doing. *Q25*

ROSIE: I think food *manufacturers* could do more to encourage healthy eating.

ADAM: How?

ROSIE: Well, <u>when manufacturers put calorie counts of a food on the label, they're sometimes really confusing and I suspect they do it</u> on purpose. Because food that's high in calories tastes better, and so they'll sell more. *Q26*

ADAM:	Yeah, so if you look at the amount of calories in a pizza, they'll give you the calories per quarter pizza and you think, oh that's not too bad. But who's going to eat a quarter pizza?	
ROSIE:	Exactly.	
ADAM:	I suppose another approach to this problem is to get people to exercise more.	
ROSIE:	Right. In England, the current guidelines are for at least 30 minutes of brisk walking, five days a week. Now when you ask them, <u>about 40% of men and 30% of women say they do this, but when you objectively measure the amount of walking they do with motion sensors, you find that only 6% of men and 4% of women do the recommended amount of exercise.</u>	*Q27*
ADAM:	Mm, so you can see why obesity is growing.	
ROSIE:	So how can people be encouraged to take more exercise?	
ADAM:	Well, for example, think of the location of stairs in a train station. <u>If people reach the stairs before they reach the escalator when they're leaving the station, they're more likely to take the stairs.</u> And <u>if you increase the *width* of the stairs, you'll get more people using them at the same time.</u> It's an unconscious process and influenced by minor modifications in their environment.	*Q28*
ROSIE:	Right. And it might not be a big change, but if it happens every day, it all adds up.	
ADAM:	Yes. But actually, <u>I'm not sure if we should be talking about exercise in our presentation.</u>	*Q29*
ROSIE:	Well, we've done quite a bit of reading about it.	
ADAM:	I know, but it's going to mean we have a very wide focus, and our tutor did say that <u>we need to focus on causes and solutions in terms of nutrition.</u>	
ROSIE:	<u>I suppose so. And we've got plenty of information about that.</u> OK, well that will be simpler.	
ADAM:	So what shall we do now? We've still got half an hour before our next lecture.	
ROSIE:	<u>Let's think about what we're going to include and what will go where.</u> Then we can decide what slides we need.	*Q30*
ADAM:	OK, fine.	

PART 4

Good morning everyone. So today we're going to look at an important creative activity and that's hand knitting. Ancient knitted garments have been found in many different countries, showing that knitting is a global activity with a long history.

When someone says the word 'knitting' <u>we might well picture an elderly person – a grandmother perhaps – sitting by the fire knitting</u> garments for themselves or other members *Q31* of the family. It's a homely image, but one that may lead you to feel that knitting is an activity of the past – and, indeed, <u>during the previous decade, it was one of the skills that was predicted to vanish</u> from everyday life. For although humans have sewn and knitted their *Q32* own clothing for a very long time, many of these craft-based skills went into decline when industrial machines took over – mainly because they were no longer passed down from one generation to another. However, that's all changing and interest in knitting classes in many countries is actually rising, as more and more people are seeking formal instruction in the skill. With that trend, we're also seeing <u>an increase in the sales figures for knitting equipment</u>. *Q33*

So why do people want to be taught to knit at a time when a machine can readily do the job for them? The answer is that knitting, as a handicraft, has numerous benefits for those doing it. Let's consider what some of these might be. While many people knitted garments in the past because they couldn't afford to buy clothes, it's still true today that <u>knitting can be helpful if you're experiencing economic hardship</u>. If you have several children who all need warm *Q34* winter clothes, knitting may save you a lot of money. And the results of knitting your own clothes can be very rewarding, even though <u>the skills you need to get going are really quite basic</u> and the financial outlay is minimal.

Q35

But the more significant benefits in today's world are to do with well-being. In a world where it's estimated that we spend up to nine hours a day online, doing something with our hands that is craft-based makes us feel good. It releases us from the stress of a technological, fast-paced life.

Now, let's look back a bit to early knitting activities. In fact, no one really knows when knitting first began, but archaeological remains have disclosed plenty of information for us to think about.

One of the interesting things about knitting is that the earliest pieces of clothing that have been found suggest that <u>most of the items produced were round</u> rather than flat. Discoveries from the 3rd and 4th centuries in Egypt show that things like socks and gloves, that were needed to keep hands and feet warm, were knitted in one piece using four or five needles. That's very different from most knitting patterns today, which only require two. What's more, the very first needles people used were hand carved out of wood and <u>other natural materials, like bone</u>, whereas today's needles are largely made of steel or plastic and make that characteristic clicking sound when someone's using them. Ancient people knitted using yarns made from linen, hemp, cotton and wool, and <u>these were often very rough on the skin</u>. The spinning wheel, which allowed people to make finer yarns and produce much greater quantities of them, led to the dominance of wool in the knitting industry – often favoured for its warmth.

Q36

Q37

Q38

Another interesting fact about knitting is that because it was practised in so many parts of the world for so many purposes, <u>regional differences in style developed</u>. This visual identity has allowed researchers to match bits of knitted clothing that have been unearthed over time to the region from which the wearer came or the job that he or she did.

Q39

As I've mentioned, knitting offered people from poor communities a way of making extra money while doing other tasks. For many centuries, it seems, men, women and children took every opportunity to knit, for example, while <u>watching over sheep</u>, walking to market or riding in boats. So, let's move on to take a …

Q40

TEST 4

PART 1

SHIRLEY: Hello?
TOM: Oh hello. I was hoping to speak to Jack Fitzgerald about renting a cottage.
SHIRLEY: I'm his wife, Shirley, and we own the cottages together, so I'm sure I can help you.
TOM: Great. My name's Tom. Some friends of ours rented Granary Cottage from you last year, and they thought it was great. So my wife and I are hoping to come in May for a week.
SHIRLEY: What date did you have in mind?
TOM: The week beginning the 14th, if possible.
SHIRLEY: I'll just check … I'm sorry, Tom, it's already booked that week. It's free the week beginning the 28th, though, for seven nights. In fact, that's the only time you could have it in May. *Q1*
TOM: Oh. Well, we could manage that, I think. We'd just need to change a couple of things. How much would it cost?
SHIRLEY: That's the beginning of high season, so it'd be £550 for the week. *Q2*
TOM: Ah. That's a bit more than we wanted to pay, I'm afraid. We've budgeted up to £500 for accommodation.
SHIRLEY: Well, we've just finished converting another building into a cottage, which we're calling Chervil Cottage. *Q3*
TOM: Sorry? What was that again?
SHIRLEY: Chervil. C-H-E-R-V for Victor I-L.
TOM: Oh, that's a herb, isn't it?
SHIRLEY: That's right. It grows fairly wild around here. You could have that for the week you want for £480.
TOM: OK. So could you tell me something about it, please?
SHIRLEY: Of course. The building was built as a garage. It's a little smaller than Granary Cottage. *Q4*
TOM: So that must sleep two people, as well?
SHIRLEY: That's right. There's a double bedroom.
TOM: Does it have a garden? *Q5*
SHIRLEY: Yes, you get to it from the living room through French doors, and we provide two deckchairs. We hope to build a patio in the near future, but I wouldn't like to guarantee it'll be finished by May.
TOM: OK.
SHIRLEY: The front door opens onto the old farmyard, and parking isn't a problem – there's plenty of room at the front for that. There are some trees and potted plants there. *Q6*

TOM: What about facilities in the cottage? It has standard things like a cooker and fridge, I presume.
SHIRLEY: In the kitchen area there's a fridge-freezer and we've just put in an electric cooker.
TOM: Is there a washing machine?
SHIRLEY: Yes. There's also a TV in the living room, which plays DVDs too. The bathroom is too small for a bath, so there's a shower instead. I think a lot of people prefer that nowadays, anyway.

TOM:	It's more environmentally friendly, isn't it? Unless you spend half the day in it!
SHIRLEY:	Exactly.
TOM:	What about heating? It sometimes gets quite cool at that time of year.
SHIRLEY:	There's central heating, and if you want to light a fire, there's a stove. We can provide all the wood you need for it. It smells so much nicer than coal, and it makes the room very cosy – we've got one in our own house.
TOM:	That sounds very pleasant. Perhaps we should come in the winter, to make the most of it!
SHIRLEY:	Yes, we find we don't want to go out when we've got the fire burning. There are some attractive views from the cottage, which I haven't mentioned. There's a famous stone bridge – it's one of the oldest in the region, and you can see it from the living room. It isn't far away. The bedroom window looks in the opposite direction, and has a lovely view of the hills and the monument at the top.
TOM:	Well, that all sounds perfect. I'd like to book it, please. Would you want a deposit?
SHIRLEY:	Yes, we ask for thirty percent to secure your booking, so that'll be, um, £144.
TOM:	And when would you like the rest of the money?
SHIRLEY:	You're coming in May, so the last day of March, please.
TOM:	Fine.
SHIRLEY:	Excellent. Could I just take your details …

Q7 at "there's a stove. We can provide all the wood you need for it." Q8 at "a famous stone bridge – it's one of the oldest". Q9 at "you can see it from the living room... The bedroom window looks in the opposite direction, and has a lovely view of the hills and the monument at the top." Q10 at "the last day of March, please."

PART 2

CHAIRPERSON:	Right. Next on the agenda we have traffic and highways. Councillor Thornton.
COUNCILLOR THORNTON:	Thank you. Well, we now have the results of the survey carried out last month about traffic and road transport in the town. People were generally satisfied with the state of the roads. There were one or two complaints about potholes which will be addressed, but a significant number of people complained about the increasing number of heavy vehicles using our local roads to avoid traffic elsewhere. We'd expected more complaints by commuters about the reduction in the train service, but it doesn't seem to have affected people too much. The cycle path that runs alongside the river is very well used by both cyclists and pedestrians since the surface was improved last year, but overtaking can be a problem so we're going to add a bit on the side to make it wider. At some stage, we'd like to extend the path so that it goes all the way through the town, but that won't be happening in the immediate future. The plans to have a pedestrian crossing next to the Post Office have unfortunately had to be put on hold for the time being. We'd budgeted for this to be done this financial year, but then there were rumours that the Post Office was going to move, which would have meant there wasn't really a need for a crossing. Now they've confirmed that they're staying where they are, but the Highways Department have told us that it would be dangerous to have a pedestrian crossing where we'd originally planned it as there's a bend in the road there. So that'll need some more thought. On Station Road near the station and level crossing, drivers can face quite long waits if the level crossing's closed, and we've now got signs up requesting them not to leave their engines running at that time. This means pedestrians waiting on the pavement to cross

Q11, Q12, Q13, Q14

the railway line don't have to breathe in car fumes. We've had some problems with cyclists leaving their bikes chained to the railings outside the ticket office, but the station has agreed to provide bike racks there.

CHAIRPERSON:
So next on the agenda is 'Proposals for improvements to the recreation ground'. Councillor Thornton again.

COUNCILLOR THORNTON:
Well, since we managed to extend the recreation ground, we've spent some time talking to local people about how it could be made a more attractive and useful space. If you have a look at the map up on the screen, you can see the river up in the north, and the Community Hall near the entrance from the road. At present, cars can park between the Community Hall and that line of trees to the east, but this is quite dangerous for pedestrians so we're suggesting a new car park on the opposite side of the Community Hall, right next to it. Q15

We also have a new location for the cricket pitch. As we've now purchased additional space to the east of the recreation ground, beyond the trees, we plan to move it away from its current location, which is rather near the road, into this new area beyond the line of trees. This means there's less danger of stray balls hitting cars or pedestrians. Q16

We've got plans for a children's playground which will be accessible by a footpath from the Community Hall and will be alongside the river. We'd originally thought of having it close to the road, but we think this will be a more attractive location. Q17

The skateboard ramp is very popular with both younger and older children – we had considered moving this up towards the river, but in the end we decided to have it in the southeast corner near the road. Q18

The pavilion is very well used at present by both football players and cricketers. It will stay where it is now – to the left of the line of trees and near to the river – handy for both the football and cricket pitches. Q19

And finally, we'll be getting a new notice board for local information, and that will be directly on people's right as they go from the road into the recreation ground. Q20

PART 3

JAKE:
Now that we've done all the research into bike-sharing schemes in cities around the world, we need to think about how we're going to organise our report.

AMY:
Right. I think we should start by talking about the benefits. I mean it's great that so many cities have introduced these schemes where anyone can pick up a bike from dozens of different locations and hire it for a few hours. It makes riding a bike very convenient for people.

JAKE:
Yes, but the costs can add up and that puts people on low incomes off in some places.

AMY:
I suppose so, but if it means more people in general are cycling rather than driving, then because they're increasing the amount of physical activity they do, it's good for their health.

JAKE:
OK. But isn't that of less importance? I mean, doesn't the impact of reduced emissions on air pollution have a more significant effect on people's health? Q21/Q22

AMY:	<u>Certainly, in some cities bike-sharing has made a big contribution to that. And</u> <u>also helped to cut the number of cars on the road significantly.</u>	*Q21/Q22*
JAKE:	<u>Which is the main point.</u>	
AMY:	<u>Exactly.</u> But I'd say it's had less of an impact on noise pollution because there are still loads of buses and lorries around.	
JAKE:	Right.	
AMY:	Shall we quickly discuss the recommendations we're going to make?	
JAKE:	In order to ensure bike-sharing schemes are successful?	
AMY:	Yes.	
JAKE:	OK. Well, while I think it's nice to have really state-of-the art bikes with things like GPS, I wouldn't say they're absolutely necessary.	
AMY:	<u>But some technical things are really important – like a fully functional app – so</u> <u>people can make payments and book bikes easily.</u> Places which haven't invested in that have really struggled.	*Q23/Q24*
JAKE:	<u>Good point</u> … Some people say there shouldn't be competing companies offering separate bike-sharing schemes, but in some really big cities, competition's beneficial and anyway one company might not be able to manage the whole thing.	
AMY:	Right. Deciding how much to invest is a big question. Cities which have opened loads of new bike lanes at the same time as introducing bike-sharing schemes have generally been more successful – but there are examples of successful schemes where this hasn't happened … <u>What does matter though – is having a</u> <u>big publicity campaign.</u>	*Q23/Q24*
JAKE:	<u>Definitely.</u> If people don't know how to use the scheme or don't understand its benefits, they won't use it. People need a lot of persuasion to stop using their cars.	

AMY:	Shall we look at some examples now? And say what we think is good or bad about them.	
JAKE:	I suppose we should start with Amsterdam as this was one of the first cities to have a bike-sharing scheme.	
AMY:	Yes. There was already a strong culture of cycling here. In a way <u>it's strange that</u> <u>there was such a demand for bike-sharing because you'd have thought most</u> <u>people would have used their own bikes.</u>	*Q25*
JAKE:	<u>And yet it's one of the best-used schemes</u> … Dublin's an interesting example of a success story.	
AMY:	<u>It must be because the public transport system's quite limited.</u>	*Q26*
JAKE:	<u>Not really</u> – there's no underground, but there are trams and <u>a good bus network.</u> <u>I'd say price has a lot to do with it.</u> It's one of the cheapest schemes in Europe to join.	
AMY:	<u>But the buses are really slow</u> – anyway the weather certainly can't be a factor!	
JAKE:	No – definitely not. The London scheme's been quite successful.	
AMY:	Yes – it's been a really good thing for the city. The bikes are popular and the whole system is well maintained but it isn't expanding quickly enough.	
JAKE:	Basically, <u>not enough's been spent on increasing the number of cycle lanes.</u> Hopefully that'll change.	*Q27*
AMY:	<u>Yes.</u> Now what about outside Europe?	
JAKE:	Well bike-sharing schemes have taken off in places like Buenos Aires.	
AMY:	Mmm. They built a huge network of cycle lanes to support the introduction of the scheme there, didn't they? It attracted huge numbers of cyclists where previously there were hardly any.	
JAKE:	<u>An example of good planning.</u>	*Q28*

AMY:	<u>Absolutely.</u> New York is a good example of how not to introduce a scheme. When they launched it, <u>it was more than ten times the price of most other schemes</u>.	
JAKE:	<u>More than it costs to take a taxi. Crazy.</u> I think the organisers lacked vision and ambition there.	*Q29*
AMY:	I think so too. Sydney would be a good example to use. <u>I would have expected it to have grown pretty quickly here.</u>	*Q30*
JAKE:	Yes. <u>I can't quite work out why it hasn't been an instant success</u> like some of the others. It's a shame really.	
AMY:	I know. OK so now we've thought about …	

PART 4

One of the most famous cases of extinction is that of a bird known as the dodo. In fact there's even a saying in English, 'as dead as the dodo', used to refer to something which no longer exists. But for many centuries the dodo was alive and well, although it could only be found in one place, the island of Mauritius in the Indian Ocean. It was a very large bird, about one metre tall, and over the centuries it had lost the ability to fly, but it survived happily under the trees that covered the island.

Then in the year 1507 the first Portuguese ships stopped at the island. The sailors were carrying <u>spices</u> back to Europe, and found the island a convenient stopping place where they could stock up with food and water for the rest of the voyage, but they didn't settle on Mauritius. However, in 1638 the Dutch arrived and set up a <u>colony</u> there. These first human inhabitants of the island found the dodo birds a convenient source of meat, although not everyone liked the taste.   *Q31* *Q32*

It's hard to get an accurate description of what the dodo actually looked like. We do have some written records from sailors, and a few pictures, but we don't know how reliable these are. The best-known picture is a Dutch painting in which the bird appears to be extremely <u>fat</u>, but this may not be accurate – an Indian painting done at the same time shows a much thinner bird.   *Q33*

Although attempts were made to preserve the bodies of some of the birds, no complete specimen survives. In the early 17th century four dried parts of a bird were known to exist – of these, three have disappeared, so only one example of soft tissue from the dodo survives, a dodo <u>head</u>. Bones have also been found, but there's only one complete skeleton in existence.   *Q34*

This single dodo skeleton has recently been the subject of scientific research which suggests that many of the earlier beliefs about dodos may have been incorrect. For example, early accounts of the birds mention how slow and clumsy it was, but scientists now believe the bird's strong knee joints would have made it capable of <u>movement</u> which was not slow, but actually quite fast. In fact, one 17th century sailor wrote that he found the birds hard to catch. It's true that the dodo's small wings wouldn't have allowed it to leave the ground, but the scientists suggest that these were probably employed for <u>balance</u> while going over uneven ground. Another group of scientists carried out analysis of the dodo's skull. They found that the reports of the lack of intelligence of the dodo were not borne out by their research, which suggested the bird's <u>brain</u> was not small, but average in size. In fact, in relation to its body size, it was similar to that of the pigeon, which is known to be a highly intelligent bird. The researchers also found that the structure of the bird's skull suggested that one sense which was particularly well-developed was that of <u>smell</u>. So the dodo may also have been particularly good at locating ripe fruit and other food in the island's thick vegetation.   *Q35* *Q36* *Q37* *Q38*

So it looks as if the dodo was better able to survive and defend itself than was originally believed. Yet less than 200 years after Europeans first arrived on the island, they had become extinct. So what was the reason for this? For a long time, it was believed that the dodos were hunted to extinction, but scientists now believe the situation was more complicated than this. Another factor may have been the new species brought to the island by the sailors. These included dogs, which would have been a threat to the dodos, and also monkeys, which ate the fruit that was the main part of the dodos' diet. These were brought to the island deliberately, but the ships also brought another type of creature – <u>rats</u>, which came to land from the ships and rapidly overran the island. These upset the ecology of the island, not just the dodos but other species too. However, they were a particular danger to the dodos because they consumed their eggs, and since each dodo only laid one at a time, this probably had a devastating effect on populations.

Q39

However, we now think that probably the main cause of the birds' extinction was not the introduction of non-native species, but the introduction of agriculture. This meant that the <u>forest</u> that had once covered all the island, and that had provided a perfect home for the dodo, was cut down so that crops such as sugar could be grown. So although the dodo had survived for thousands of years, suddenly it was gone.

Q40

Listening and Reading answer keys

TEST 1

LISTENING

 Answer key with extra explanations in Resource Bank

Part 1, Questions 1–10

1 egg
2 tower
3 car
4 animals
5 bridge
6 movie / film
7 decorate
8 Wednesdays
9 Fradstone
10 parking

Part 2, Questions 11–20

11 C
12 A
13 B
14 C
15 H
16 C
17 G
18 B
19 I
20 A

Part 3, Questions 21–30

21&22 *IN EITHER ORDER*
       C
       E
23&24 *IN EITHER ORDER*
       B
       E
25 D
26 C
27 A
28 H
29 F
30 G

Part 4, Questions 31–40

31 practical
32 publication
33 choices
34 negative
35 play
36 capitalism
37 depression
38 logic
39 opportunity
40 practice / practise

If you score …

1–17	18–27	28–40
you are unlikely to get an acceptable score under examination conditions and we recommend that you spend a lot of time improving your English before you take IELTS.	you may get an acceptable score under examination conditions but we recommend that you think about having more practice or lessons before you take IELTS.	you are likely to get an acceptable score under examination conditions but remember that different institutions will find different scores acceptable.

TEST 1

READING

 Answer key with extra explanations in Resource Bank

Reading Passage 1, Questions 1–13

1 FALSE
2 FALSE
3 NOT GIVEN
4 TRUE
5 TRUE
6 FALSE
7 TRUE
8 violent
9 tool
10 meat
11 photographer
12 game
13 frustration

Reading Passage 2, Questions 14–26

14 iv
15 vii
16 ii
17 v
18 i
19 viii
20 vi
21 city
22 priests
23 trench
24 location
25&26 *IN EITHER ORDER*
  B
  D

Reading Passage 3, Questions 27–40

27 B
28 D
29 C
30 D
31 G
32 E
33 C
34 F
35 B
36 A
37 C
38 A
39 B
40 C

If you score …

1–17	18–25	26–40
you are unlikely to get an acceptable score under examination conditions and we recommend that you spend a lot of time improving your English before you take IELTS.	you may get an acceptable score under examination conditions but we recommend that you think about having more practice or lessons before you take IELTS.	you are likely to get an acceptable score under examination conditions but remember that different institutions will find different scores acceptable.

TEST 2

LISTENING

 Answer key with extra explanations in Resource Bank

Part 1, Questions 1–10

1 frame
2 195
3 payment
4 Grandparents
5 colour / color
6 hand
7 background
8 focus
9 ten / 10 days
10 plastic

Part 2, Questions 11–20

11 C
12 B
13 A
14 A
15 C
16 D
17 A
18 B
19&20 *IN EITHER ORDER*
    B
    C

Part 3, Questions 21–30

21 B
22 A
23 C
24 C
25 history
26 paper
27 humans / people
28 stress
29 graph
30 evaluate

Part 4, Questions 31–40

31 creativity
32 therapy
33 fitness
34 balance
35 brain
36 motivation
37 isolation
38 calories
39 obesity
40 habit

If you score …

1–18	19–28	29–40
you are unlikely to get an acceptable score under examination conditions and we recommend that you spend a lot of time improving your English before you take IELTS.	you may get an acceptable score under examination conditions but we recommend that you think about having more practice or lessons before you take IELTS.	you are likely to get an acceptable score under examination conditions but remember that different institutions will find different scores acceptable.

TEST 2

READING

 Answer key with extra explanations in Resource Bank

Reading Passage 1, Questions 1–13

1 TRUE
2 NOT GIVEN
3 TRUE
4 FALSE
5 FALSE
6 TRUE
7 TRUE
8 NOT GIVEN
9 Ridgeway
10 documents
11 soil
12 fertility
13 Rhiannon

Reading Passage 2, Questions 14–26

14 D
15 C
16 A
17 G
18 B
19 H
20 E
21 YES
22 NO
23 NOT GIVEN
24 YES
25 NOT GIVEN
26 NO

Reading Passage 3, Questions 27–40

27 B
28 C
29 B
30 D
31 D
32 A
33 C
34 F
35 G
36 FALSE
37 NOT GIVEN
38 NOT GIVEN
39 TRUE
40 TRUE

If you score …

1–17	18–25	26–40
you are unlikely to get an acceptable score under examination conditions and we recommend that you spend a lot of time improving your English before you take IELTS.	you may get an acceptable score under examination conditions but we recommend that you think about having more practice or lessons before you take IELTS.	you are likely to get an acceptable score under examination conditions but remember that different institutions will find different scores acceptable.

TEST 3

LISTENING

 Answer key with extra explanations in Resource Bank

Part 1, Questions 1–10

1	park
2	blue
3	reference
4	story
5	rain
6	snack
7	medication
8	helmet
9	tent
10	199

Part 2, Questions 11–20

11&12 *IN EITHER ORDER*
    A
    C
13&14 *IN EITHER ORDER*
    B
    C
15 D
16 F
17 A
18 H
19 C
20 G

Part 3, Questions 21–30

21&22 *IN EITHER ORDER*
    C
    D
23&24 *IN EITHER ORDER*
    C
    E
25 C
26 A
27 B
28 A
29 A
30 C

Part 4, Questions 31–40

31	grandmother
32	decade
33	equipment
34	economic
35	basic
36	round
37	bone
38	rough
39	style
40	sheep

If you score …

1–18	19–27	28–40
you are unlikely to get an acceptable score under examination conditions and we recommend that you spend a lot of time improving your English before you take IELTS.	you may get an acceptable score under examination conditions but we recommend that you think about having more practice or lessons before you take IELTS.	you are likely to get an acceptable score under examination conditions but remember that different institutions will find different scores acceptable.

TEST 3

READING

 Answer key with extra explanations in Resource Bank

Reading Passage 1, Questions 1–13

1   FALSE
2   NOT GIVEN
3   FALSE
4   TRUE
5   TRUE
6   lightweight
7   bronze
8   levels
9   hull
10 triangular
11 music
12 grain
13 towboats

Reading Passage 2, Questions 14–26

14 D
15 C
16 F
17 H
18 G
19 B
20 microorganisms / micro-organisms
21 reindeer

22 insects
23&24 *IN EITHER ORDER*
       B
       C
25&26 *IN EITHER ORDER*
       A
       C

Reading Passage 3, Questions 27–40

27 NOT GIVEN
28 TRUE
29 TRUE
30 NOT GIVEN
31 FALSE
32 FALSE
33 H
34 D
35 G
36 C
37 A
38 warm (winter)
39 summer
40 mustard plant(s) / mustard

If you score ...

1–17	18–26	27–40
you are unlikely to get an acceptable score under examination conditions and we recommend that you spend a lot of time improving your English before you take IELTS.	you may get an acceptable score under examination conditions but we recommend that you think about having more practice or lessons before you take IELTS.	you are likely to get an acceptable score under examination conditions but remember that different institutions will find different scores acceptable.

TEST 4

LISTENING

 Answer key with extra explanations in Resource Bank

Part 1, Questions 1–10

1   28th
2   550
3   Chervil
4   garage
5   garden
6   parking
7   wood
8   bridge
9   monument
10 March

Part 2, Questions 11–20

11 C
12 A
13 B
14 B
15 C
16 F
17 A
18 I
19 E
20 H

Part 3, Questions 21–30

21&22 *IN EITHER ORDER*
       B
       C
23&24 *IN EITHER ORDER*
       B
       C
25 C
26 F
27 D
28 E
29 B
30 A

Part 4, Questions 31–40

31 spice(s)
32 colony / settlement
33 fat
34 head
35 movement
36 balance / balancing
37 brain
38 smell
39 rats
40 forest

If you score ...

1–18	19–27	28–40
you are unlikely to get an acceptable score under examination conditions and we recommend that you spend a lot of time improving your English before you take IELTS.	you may get an acceptable score under examination conditions but we recommend that you think about having more practice or lessons before you take IELTS.	you are likely to get an acceptable score under examination conditions but remember that different institutions will find different scores acceptable.

TEST 4

READING

 Answer key with extra explanations
in Resource Bank

Reading Passage 1,
Questions 1–13

1	posts
2	canal
3	ventilation
4	lid
5	weight
6	climbing
7	FALSE
8	NOT GIVEN
9	FALSE
10	TRUE
11	gold
12	(the) architect('s) (name)
13	(the) harbour / harbor

Reading Passage 2,
Questions 14–26

14	A
15	B
16	D
17	B
18	D
19	H
20	F
21	B

22	C
23	YES
24	NO
25	NOT GIVEN
26	YES

Reading Passage 3,
Questions 27–40

27	iii
28	vi
29	ii
30	i
31	vii
32	v
33	C
34	B
35	A
36	NO
37	NOT GIVEN
38	YES
39	NO
40	YES

If you score …

1–16	17–25	26–40
you are unlikely to get an acceptable score under examination conditions and we recommend that you spend a lot of time improving your English before you take IELTS.	you may get an acceptable score under examination conditions but we recommend that you think about having more practice or lessons before you take IELTS.	you are likely to get an acceptable score under examination conditions but remember that different institutions will find different scores acceptable.

Sample Writing answers

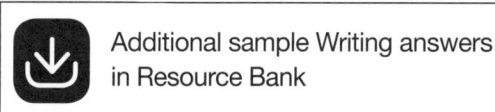 Additional sample Writing answers in Resource Bank

TEST 1, WRITING TASK 1

This is an answer written by a candidate who achieved a **Band 5.0** score.

This charts shows about percentage of households with electrical appliances and Number of hour at housework per week, per household between 1920 and 2019.

In the first chart washing machine. Refrigerator. Vacuum cleaner all rise from 1920 to 2019. Refrigerator and Vacuum cleaner increase faster than washing machine. In 1920, Refrigerator just zero percentage of households and Refrigerator is 30 percentage of households, but in 2019 they all increase 100 percentage of household. Washing machine is to percantage of households in 1920, however in 2019 is just increase about 15 percantage at households, and washing mashine is overed by Pefrigerator and Vacuum cleaner in 1940 and 1960. Vacuum cleaner is overed by Pefrigerator in 1942.

In the second chart Houses per week is 50 Number of hours per week, but it decline to 10 Number of hours per week in 2019.

Over than, percentang of households with electical appliance increase however Number of hours per week decline from 1920 to 2019.

Here is the examiner's comment:

> This is an attempt to present the information from both graphs. However, there is inaccurate data, e.g. washing machine use increased by 15%. It actually increased from 40% in 1920 to just over 70% in 2019. The response focuses on the detail of when the lines on the graph intersect but there is a lack of clarity in these details. The description of the second chart lacks detail. This limits the task achievement. There is an attempt to present the information in order, and the last line attempts an overview. However, there is a lack of coherence caused by missing or inaccurate cohesive features [*Over than*] and there is repetition [percentage of household | number of hours per week] caused by the lack of cohesion.
>
> Vocabulary is minimally adequate for the task but there are errors in word choice [*overed by* / overtaken by] which mean the response is difficult to understand. The frequency of errors in spelling is also high [*percantage* / *percentang* / percentage | *mashine* / machine | *Pefrigerator* / refrigerator | *electical* / electrical]. The range of grammatical structures is limited. There are some correct examples [*all rise from 1920 to 2019* | *they all increase (to) 100 percentage*]; however, the errors in grammar and punctuation mean the response is not clear.

TEST 1, WRITING TASK 2

This is an answer written by a candidate who achieved a **Band 6.0** score.

In our rather futuristic society for a number of reasons people are getting more interested in the past of their hometowns. With the help of rapidly ameliorating technology their desire to learn about the history can be easily put into life. But what are the roots of such an eagerness?

First of all, the hectic lifestyle that we all experience nowadays does not leave any space for calmness and peace in our souls, so most of the people – especially adolescence – are struggling with finding their feet, whilst having a broad spectrum of knowledge about the world around really gives a feeling of confidence in the impermanence of life. In addition to this, it is said that being aware of the past you can change the future. Consequently, if people want to live a better life in more comfortable environment, they have to explore the history of their homes in order not to repeat past mistakes.

For this aims we are lucky to have multiple tools to carry out research into the subject. Despite libraries being considered as an old-fashioned and not necessarily convinient approach of learning, there are actually quite a few books and magazines which are not available online but which are extremely helpful when it comes to the local interests. News, photos, articles and interviews with different people published in old magazines indeed provide with a clear image of past events. Brousing the internet forums is also a great idea to find new information and make friend with mutual objectives.

Putting everything into a nutshell, learning about the history of your place not only builds a sense of confidence but also might have a big impact on our future way of life.

Here is the examiner's comment:

> This response provides a range of ideas on the value of knowing about history, but not specifically about the history of houses or buildings people live in. The main points are addressed but the ideas that relate directly to the question are limited.
>
> The response is organised into four paragraphs, with an introduction and conclusion. Each main paragraph covers one of the points in the question, but the lack of focus means that there is a lack of overall progression. Cohesive devices are used well [*First of all | Consequently*] but there are some errors [*For this aims*].
>
> Vocabulary is the strongest part of this response, with some examples of higher-level collocation [*hectic lifestyle | peace in our souls | finding their feet | broad spectrum of knowledge | impermanence of life | mutual objectives*]. There are a variety of sentence structures but errors remain.
>
> To improve this response, the candidate should refer more closely to the 'house or building' rather than the hometown.

TEST 2, WRITING TASK 1

This is an answer written by a candidate who achieved a **Band 6.0** score.

The diagram illustrates the process by which sugar is produced from sugar cane. The process consists of seven steps of various time length, starting by farming sugar canes and ending by dry sugar ready to use.

First, sugarcane is farmed and nurished for a period of 12 to 18 months, which is the longest step in the whole process. Second, sugar cane get harvested by the means of two ways, either manually or using specialized vehicles. Third, the harvested sugar cane go through the step of crushing, resulting in liquid form called juice.

The fourth step involves purifying the juice through Limestone filters. The purified juice now goes through the fifth step, which put it under extreme heat to allow it to evaporate to get syrup out from it. Then the syrup is centrifuged to separate sugar crystals from syrup. Once that happend the sugar is taken into the last phase of drying and cooling, which finalise the process and produce ready-to-use sugar that is packed and ready for sale.

Here is the examiner's comment:

> There is an overview presented in the first paragraph which summarises the process into the farming stages and the drying stages. This summary could be more detailed, e.g. farming, crushing, separating and drying stages. The ideas are presented in three paragraphs and follow the logical sequence of the process. Cohesive devices are basic [*First* | *Second* | *Third* | *fourth*] and there is some repetition, but there is a clear progression.
>
> Spelling is generally accurate and the vocabulary conveys the message well, with some range [*the longest step* | *specialized vehicles* | *liquid*]. Grammatical range is weaker and there are a number of errors [*get harvested* / is harvested] including third-person endings [*go through* / goes through | *put* / puts].
>
> This response could be improved by a more detailed overview and more accuracy in grammatical structures.

TEST 2, WRITING TASK 2

This is an answer written by a candidate who achieved a **Band 4.5** score.

In their advertising, businesses nowdays sometimes stress that their products are new in some way. From my point of view, some businesses want to have good products to give to the people, but usually they worry about their products are newer than some other's businesses products.

In think it is a negative development, because when businesses stress about the quality of their products, sometimes they do something wrong while they are producing them. It is good when the businesses take care of and look after their products but with a limit. According to some experts, when you take a lot of care of something, you will probably do some things, about it, wrong.

From my own experience, I was trying to make three school projects, which my teachers asked me to do, and despite my hard work and because I was stressed about the projects I had to do, I finally failed because I had made a lot of mistakes.

To sum up, businesses nowdays should not stress about their products being new in some way. Besides that they should calm down and be careful on what they are producing.

Here is the examiner's comment:

This response does not really address the requirements of the question. There is a view expressed at the beginning of the second paragraph [*a negative development*] but mainly, the writer is talking about the quality of products rather than advertising. In the third paragraph, an example is given about an unsuccessful school project which is not relevant to the question either. This response only touches on the question set, and is a tangential response. Ideas are not arranged coherently, as they do not address the task given. Paragraphing is not helpful and there is a one-sentence paragraph. Vocabulary is not appropriate as it does not focus on the question set.

Sentence structure shows a mix of simple and more complex forms with a range of tenses and modal and comparative structures. There are a number of errors but they do not reduce communication.

TEST 3, WRITING TASK 1

This is an answer written by a candidate who achieved a **Band 6.5** score.

The South West airport had some changes after its redevelopment. The departures area was modified to have a bag drop service, along with a cafe and check-in module that were already there before the redevelopment. However, both the cafe and the check-in module changed places to make room for the bag drop. After going through security passport control, passengers and airport staff will be able to purchase stuff at the new stores before their flight. After doing some shopping, the boarding gates wait ahead. There are now 18 gates, which were 8 before the redevelopment. For this reason, the walkaway installed between the gates has been replaced for a sky train, which will be able to transport people along the different gates. But if you're not leaving the South West airport, you'll be glad to know the arrivals area has also been redeveloped. After going through passport control customs, passengers and airport staff will be able to hire different services. This area was empty before the redevelopment, but now it has an ATM, a cafe and a car hire service that will gladly take you to your destination.

Here is the examiner's comment:

> This response covers the key details required; however, it describes the changes in the past tense instead of using future verb forms for the development 'next year'. Overall, it could be improved by adding a summary of the main changes.

> The response has been organised logically by describing the changes to the journey through the redeveloped airport: firstly departures, then arrivals. There are some good cohesive features [*However | After | But*] and some referencing [*which | This area*]. Organisation could be improved by breaking the response down into two or three paragraphs.

> Vocabulary is a strength, with some effective collocation [*changed places | take you to your destination*] and flexibility [*modified | installed between*].

> In terms of grammar, this response has a variety of structures, but it describes some of the changes in the past simple [*was modified*] and in the present perfect [*has been replaced by*] whereas the question asked for a description of the future changes. To improve the score, there should be a wider range of future structures to address the changes 'next year'.

TEST 3, WRITING TASK 2

This is an answer written by a candidate who achieved a **Band 7.0** score.

Today high levels of sugar are contained in many sources of food, especially in manufactured food. And, of course, eating so much sugar is not good for our health: it can cause just a simple cavy, for example, but also worse problems, like the increasing level of sugar in blood. Some people suggest that sugary products should be more expensive, so people would buy less of them.

According to me, I think that this solution is not the best one as sugary products include some types of food that we eat everyday, such as bread or pasta. This foods, particularly the first one, are really important in our diet, so make them more expensive will influence not only our lifestyle, but also some people wouldn't be able anymore to buy the most important food for them. Just think for example to poor people, who can maybe afford a few loads of bread per day: what would they eat if we increased bread price?

I think that the best solution for this problem would be informing people about what they eat, because sometimes we don't even know that. They have already done something to inform people about the characteristics of food, of course, and lebels are one of the most important thing, as they tell you all the ingredients of a particular food. Yet, not many people spend some of their time reading lebels, or, if they do it, they probably don't know the biggest part of the substances named in the list, as well not everybody knows that there is a specific order of the ingredients in the list. So something we could do is organizing some "talks" to inform people not only about the function of lebels, but especially about the big amount of sugar we eat everyday. I think as well that this talks should be organised also in schools, because also children must be aware of what they eat; besides, children can tell what they have learned by these "conferences" at their parents, so the whole family would eat better.

To sum it up, I think that it is not necessary to increase the prices of sugary food and that all we need is information, that will lead people to eat less sugary food and, as a consequence, live better with less problems.

Here is the examiner's comment:

> This is a good response to the question. It does not agree with the statement and presents a different solution to the problem.
>
> There are four paragraphs, made up of an introduction, a conclusion and two further paragraphs explaining why the candidate disagrees with the statement and then giving an alternative solution. Ideas are logically organised, with a range of linking devices to make the response easier to read [*Yet* | *as well* | *I think as well that* | *as a consequence*], but there are some errors [*This* / these | *also*].
>
> There are 386 words in this response, well over the expected 250 words. In this case, the increased wordcount results in a good range of vocabulary with some flexibility and collocation [*informing people about what they eat* | *aware of what they eat*] despite some remaining errors [*cavy* / cavity | *lebels* / labels].
>
> The response uses a variety of structures [*what would they eat if we increased bread price?*] despite some errors [*by these "conferences"* / at these "conferences" | *less problems* / fewer problems].

TEST 4, WRITING TASK 1

This is an answer written by a candidate who achieved a **Band 5.5** score.

Plastic bottles are one of the most materials used in the world, and recycling is a really important subject to try to minimize the waste.

Around the streets, in front off houses and restaurants is possible to see some bins, to collect organic and recycle waste. The yellow in is the correct one to trash recycle things, such as plastic bottles. After trashed, a truck collects at least once a week and leave in a specific place to separate what is recycleble and what is not. For that reason, is really important to separate before trash, this means someone will not spend to many time separating.

Recycling is a big process, after separated the waste should be compressing in blocks to facilitat the crushing and washing process, that should be done because to many durty come with the bottles and crushing it makes easier to produce a new material.

Crushed, washed and then going to the production of plastic pellets, it is can be finally heated to form a raw material.

But what can be produced using recycled bottles? New bottles, containers, bags, T-shirts, pen, toys and to many other things.

Searching, it is possible to see how big is the waste problem around the world and how not to many govermnents invests in this situation. Starting into the houses, avoiding to use plastics in excess and separating the correct things in the correct bins, is a good way to keep the environment safe.

Here is the examiner's comment:

> In this process task, the response includes an introduction and covers the main stages of the recycling process. However, there is significant irrelevant detail included, e.g. in the last paragraph, which reduces the score.

> The stages are set out in order and there is good overall progression with some effective linking devices [*such as* | *For that reason*] and cohesion [*what is … what is not* | *that*] but the errors reduce the band score here. The candidate tends to use lists rather than a full range of cohesive devices.

> Vocabulary is adequate with some original vocabulary [*minimize the waste* | *separated* | *containers* | *environment*]; however, much is taken directly from the task [*compressing* | *to form a raw material*]. There are errors in spelling [*in* / bin | *durty* / dirty] but they do not reduce communication.

> Grammatical structures are limited and level of error is high [*after separated* / after separating | *should be compressing* / should be compressed | *it is can be* / it can be]. For a higher score, improved accuracy is needed.

> The score for this response could be improved by including a summary of the main stages of the process, e.g. plastic bottles are collected, sorted, broken down and made into new products.

TEST 4, WRITING TASK 2

This is an answer written by a candidate who achieved a **Band 4.0** score.

The Advanteg of Driveles Vehicles

First of all number of vehicles is incarese day after day which means ever day the world gets more drivers then before. If we admite that alots of people prefer to use public transport we do not have any doubts that many people use the vehicles because of advantags of driving.

The history shows us that the human like to move from place to another for many reasns and the always fell pleased when the rid. This days people have all kind of vehicles bicks, cars, motor...etc because they all have a different advantage.

people needs also can not meet at be found in one pleace for that reason people need to move from a pleace to another place to meet thier needs which means the advantage of moving from point to anther point will be exist for ever.

World has bee changed a lot and many people have got great jobs with big salaries. The can easly fund thier vehicl and because people get feeling boring if the used to some thing they always perefer to chang thier vehicle from time to time.

Finally I think it is very hard to believe that the driverless vehicles with outweigh the disadvantages because people always find drive more and more give thier life meaning and add more advantage to it all kind of vehicles give happeness to a lot of people that they can not think about lossing it

Here is the examiner's comment:

> Most of the ideas in this response are not relevant to the question. It mainly talks about the need people have to go from place to place and how people like different types of transport. However, there is a position expressed in the final paragraph. A title is not required in Task 2.

> There is some attempt to organise the ideas and there are some basic cohesive devices [*First of all | Finally*], but there is inaccuracy and a general lack of coherence. There is no clear progression.

> There is a high density of error in the use of vocabulary in terms of spelling and word choice [*easly fund thier vehicl | perefer to chang thier*]. Sentence structures are very limited, although there are some attempts at subordinate clauses [*because they all have a different advantage*].

Sample answer sheets

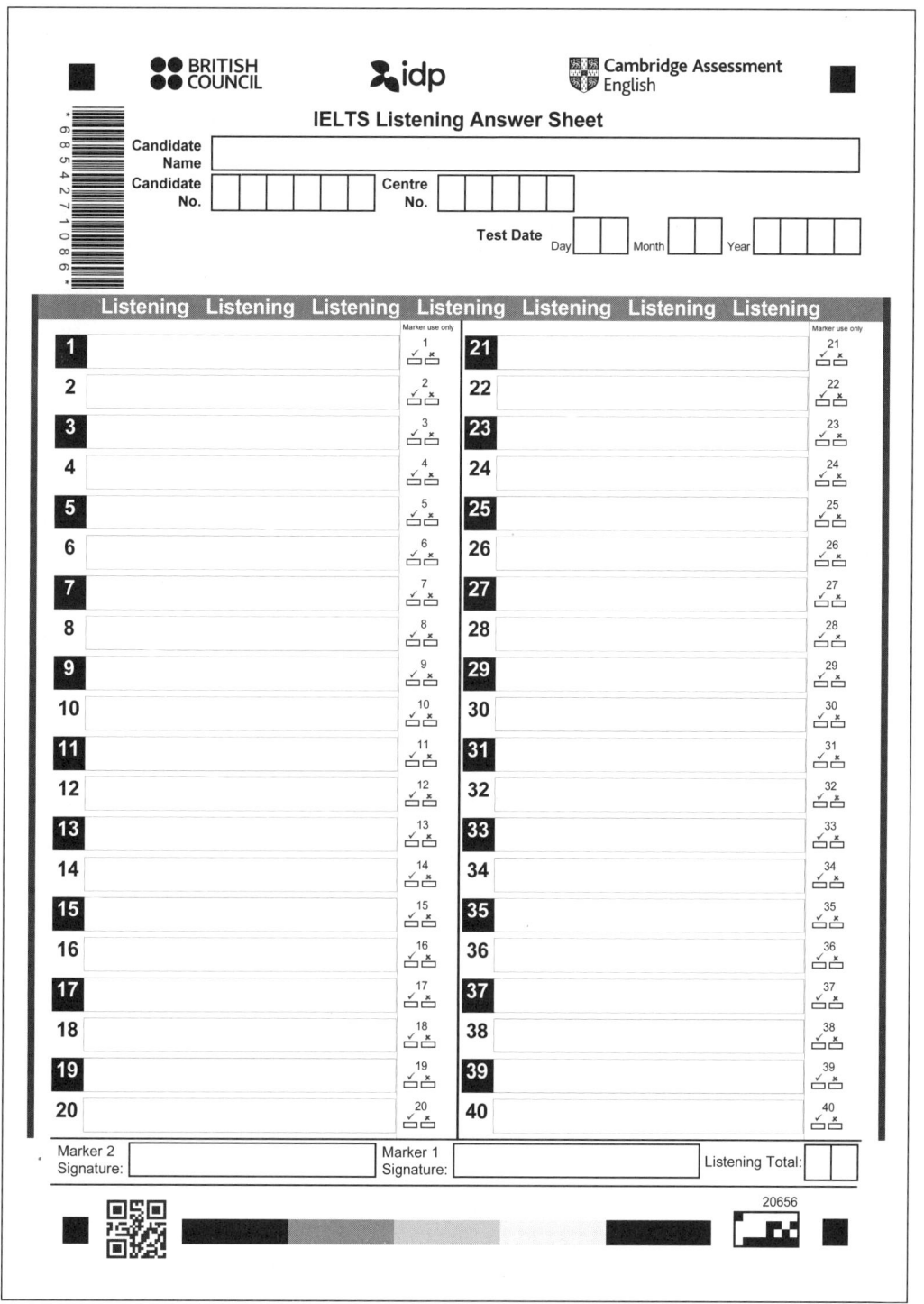

Sample answer sheets

BRITISH COUNCIL   **idp**   **Cambridge Assessment English**

IELTS Reading Answer Sheet

Candidate Name	

Candidate No.							Centre No.						

Test Module	☐ Academic ☐ General Training	Test Date	Day [ ][ ] Month [ ][ ] Year [ ][ ][ ][ ]

Reading   Reading   Reading   Reading   Reading   Reading   Reading

	Marker use only			Marker use only
1	1 ✓ ✗	**21**	21 ✓ ✗
2	2 ✓ ✗	22	22 ✓ ✗
3	3 ✓ ✗	**23**	23 ✓ ✗
4	4 ✓ ✗	24	24 ✓ ✗
5	5 ✓ ✗	**25**	25 ✓ ✗
6	6 ✓ ✗	26	26 ✓ ✗
7	7 ✓ ✗	**27**	27 ✓ ✗
8	8 ✓ ✗	28	28 ✓ ✗
9	9 ✓ ✗	**29**	29 ✓ ✗
10	10 ✓ ✗	30	30 ✓ ✗
11	11 ✓ ✗	**31**	31 ✓ ✗
12	12 ✓ ✗	32	32 ✓ ✗
13	13 ✓ ✗	**33**	33 ✓ ✗
14	14 ✓ ✗	34	34 ✓ ✗
15	15 ✓ ✗	**35**	35 ✓ ✗
16	16 ✓ ✗	36	36 ✓ ✗
17	17 ✓ ✗	**37**	37 ✓ ✗
18	18 ✓ ✗	38	38 ✓ ✗
19	19 ✓ ✗	**39**	39 ✓ ✗
20	20 ✓ ✗	40	40 ✓ ✗

Marker 2 Signature:	Marker 1 Signature:	Reading Total: [ ][ ]

61788

BRITISH COUNCIL

idp

Cambridge Assessment English

IELTS Writing Answer Sheet - TASK 1

Candidate Name

Candidate No.

Centre No.

Test Module ☐ Academic ☐ General Training

Test Date Day Month Year

If you need more space to write your answer, use an additional sheet and write in the space provided to indicate how many sheets you are using: Sheet ☐ of ☐

Writing Task 1 Writing Task 1 Writing Task 1 Writing Task 1

Do not write below this line

Do not write in this area. Please continue your answer on the other side of this sheet.

23505

Sample answer sheets

idp

Cambridge Assessment
English

IELTS Writing Answer Sheet - TASK 2

Candidate Name	
Candidate No.	Centre No.
Test Module	☐ Academic ☐ General Training

Test Date Day ☐ Month ☐ Year ☐

If you need more space to write your answer, use an additional sheet and write in the space provided to indicate how many sheets you are using: Sheet ☐ of ☐

Writing Task 2 Writing Task 2 Writing Task 2 Writing Task 2

Do not write below this line

Do not write in this area. Please continue your answer on the other side of this sheet.

39507

Acknowledgements

The authors and publishers acknowledge the following sources of copyright material and are grateful for the permissions granted. While every effort has been made, it has not always been possible to identify the sources of all the material used, or to trace all copyright holders. If any omissions are brought to our notice, we will be happy to include the appropriate acknowledgements on reprinting and in the next update to the digital edition, as applicable.

Key: L = Listening, R = Reading, W = Writing

Text

L1: Ryan Holiday for the adapted text from 'Stoicism: Practical Philosophy You Can Actually Use' by Ryan Holiday. Copyright © Ryan Holiday. Reproduced with kind permission; **R1:** Rachael Beasley for the adapted text from 'Why care about the Polar Bear?' by Rachael Beasley, February 2018. Copyright © Rachael Beasley. Reproduced with kind permission; Ancient History Encyclopedia for the adapted text from 'Step Pyramid of Djoser' by Joshua J. Mark, 14.02.2016. Copyright © Ancient History Encyclopedia. Reproduced with permission; University of Cambridge for the adapted text from 'Future of work'. Copyright © University of Cambridge. Reproduced with kind permission; **R2:** Ancient History Encyclopedia for the adapted text from 'The White Horse of Uffington' by Brian Haughton, 30.03.2011. Copyright © Ancient History Encyclopedia. Reproduced with permission; Literary Review for the adapted text from 'I Contain Multitudes: The Microbes Within Us and a Grander View of Life' by Ed Yong. Copyright © Literary Review. Reproduced with kind permission; Association for Psychological Science for the adapted text from 'The Factors That Foster Wise Reasoning'. This story first appeared as an April 17 Observation, a membership blog of the Association for Psychological Science. Copyright © Association for Psychological Science. Reproduced with kind permission; **R3:** Ancient History Encyclopedia for the adapted text from 'Roman Shipbuilding' by Victor Labate, 06.03.2017. Copyright © Ancient History Encyclopedia. Reproduced with permission; Kiona N. Smith for the adapted text from 'Climate change melting pre-Viking artifacts out of Norway's glaciers' by Kiona N. Smith. Copyright © Kiona N. Smith. Reproduced with kind permission; **R4:** Ancient History Encyclopedia for the adapted text from 'Roman Tunnels' by Victor Labate, 06.04.2016. Copyright © Ancient History Encyclopedia. Reproduced with permission; The Guardian for the adapted text from 'Skim reading is the new normal. The effect on society is profound' by Maryanne Wolf, *The Guardian*, 25.08.2018. Copyright © 2020 Guardian News & Media Ltd. Reproduced with permission; Vyacheslav Polonski for the adapted text from 'People don't trust AI – here's how we can change that', by Vyacheslav Polonski, 10.01.2018. Copyright © Vyacheslav Polonski. Reproduced with permission; **W2:** European Food Information Council for the figure based on 'Sugar: How is it produced from cane?' 07.10.2015, *EUFIC.org.* Copyright © European Food Information Council. Reproduced with kind permission; **W3:** Diagram of Southwest Airport courtesy of Qantas Group. Reproduced with kind permission.

Illustration

Illustrations commissioned by Cambridge Assessment

Audio

Audio production by dsound recording studios

Typesetting

Typeset by QBS Learning

URLs

The publisher has used its best endeavours to ensure that the URLs for external websites referred to in this book are correct and active at the time of going to press. However, the publisher has no responsibility for the websites and can make no guarantee that a site will remain live or that the content is or will remain appropriate